THE MONASTERY OF ALCOBAÇA

THE MONASTERY OF ALCOBAÇA

JORGE RODRIGUES

© Instituto Português do Património Arquitectónico (IPPAR)
and Scala Publishers, 2007

First published in 2007 by Scala Publishers Ltd
Northburgh House
10 Northburgh Street
London EC1V OAT

ISBN-10: 1 85759 310 3
ISBN-13: 978 1 85759 310 5

AUTHOR
Jorge Rodrigues
Text translated from the Portuguese by Gilla Evans and Isabel Varea

EDITORIAL CO-ORDINATION
Manuel Lacerda (DE/IPPAR), Miguel Soromenho (DE/IPPAR),
Sandra Pisano (Scala Publishers), in collaboration with:
Rui Rasquilho (Monastery of Alcobaça/IPPAR),
Isabel Costeira (Monastery of Alcobaça/IPPAR),
Antonio José Cruz (DE/IPPAR), Filipe Costa

EDITORIAL ASSISTANCE
Dulce de Freitas Ferraz (DCD/IPPAR),
António Ferreira Gomes (DCD/IPPAR)

DESIGN
Nigel Soper

PRINTED in Spain
10 9 8 7 6 5 4 3 2 1

PHOTOGRAPHIC CREDITS
All photographs by Mariano Piçarra except:
IPPAR/Henrique Ruas pages 2, 6, 10, 19, 24, 44 left, 53, 55,
67 top, 70-71, 106, 107, 108, 109, 110, 111, 112, 114, 115, 120, 121;
IPPAR/Luís Pavão back cover, page 94;
Circulo de Leitores page 48

Plan: © IPPAR, Maria João Saldanha/De visu

Previous page
The Cloister of Silence
and the north wall of the church

CONTENTS

Foreword	7
Plan	8
The Foundation of the Monastery	11
Cistercian Monasteries in Portugal	15
The Monastery of Alcobaça	21
The Church	25
The Cloister of Silence	55
The Chapter House	65
The Parlour	69
The Monks' Hall	69
The Kitchen	73
The Refectory	77
The Monks' Dormitory	81
The Pantheon	91
The Hall of the Kings	95
The New Wings	107
The Seventeenth-Century Additions	109
The Woodcutting Cloister	113
The Library	117
The Obelisk Garden	119
The Myrtle Garden and Chapel of Exile	123
Bibliography	128

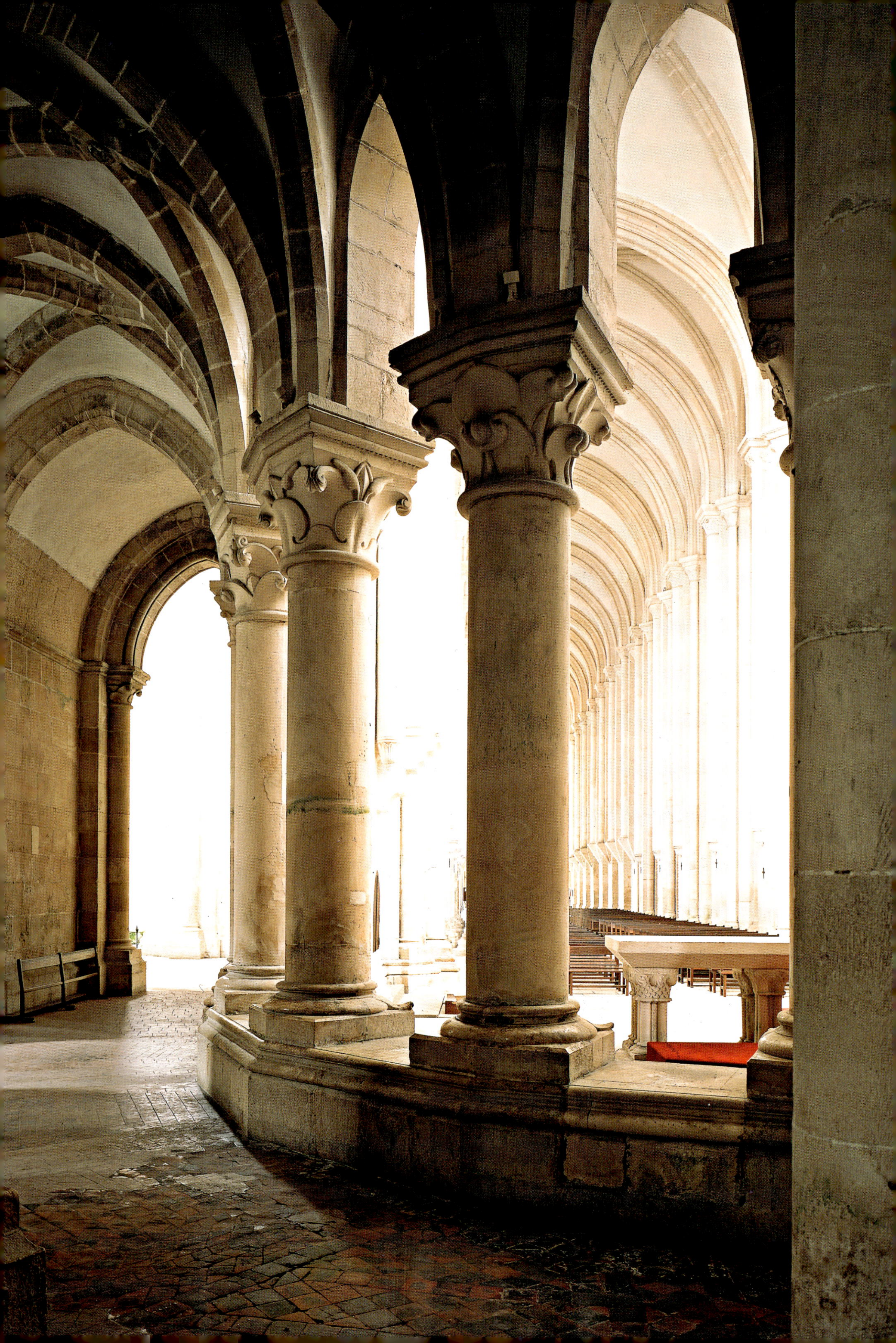

The chancel
and ambulatory

FOREWORD

The Monastery of Alcobaça, which was added to UNESCO's World Heritage List in 1989, is the most important Cistercian monument in Portugal and one of the most significant in Europe.

The building we see today testifies to the Cistercian Order's long history in Portugal, where its members have been present for nearly 700 years. We are able to appreciate how the architects and craftsmen of different eras contributed to this magnificent complex, which has had a profound effect on the development of Portugal. Beginning with a central nucleus modelled on the mother-house at Clairvaux, the monastery expanded through the centuries, reflecting the values and the technical and artistic achievements of each period, and growing rich with layers of meaning that are fascinating to decode.

This guidebook is designed to add enjoyment to your visit to this exceptional place which, while playing an active role in our contemporary world, still offers sensory experiences of structure, light and silence that evoke bygone ages. It is also our intention that this book will increase the visitor's knowledge of the history of the monastery and of the many examples of artistry to be found here.

Elísio Summavielle
President of the Instituto Português do Património Arquitectónico (IPPAR)

8　The Monastery of Alcobaça

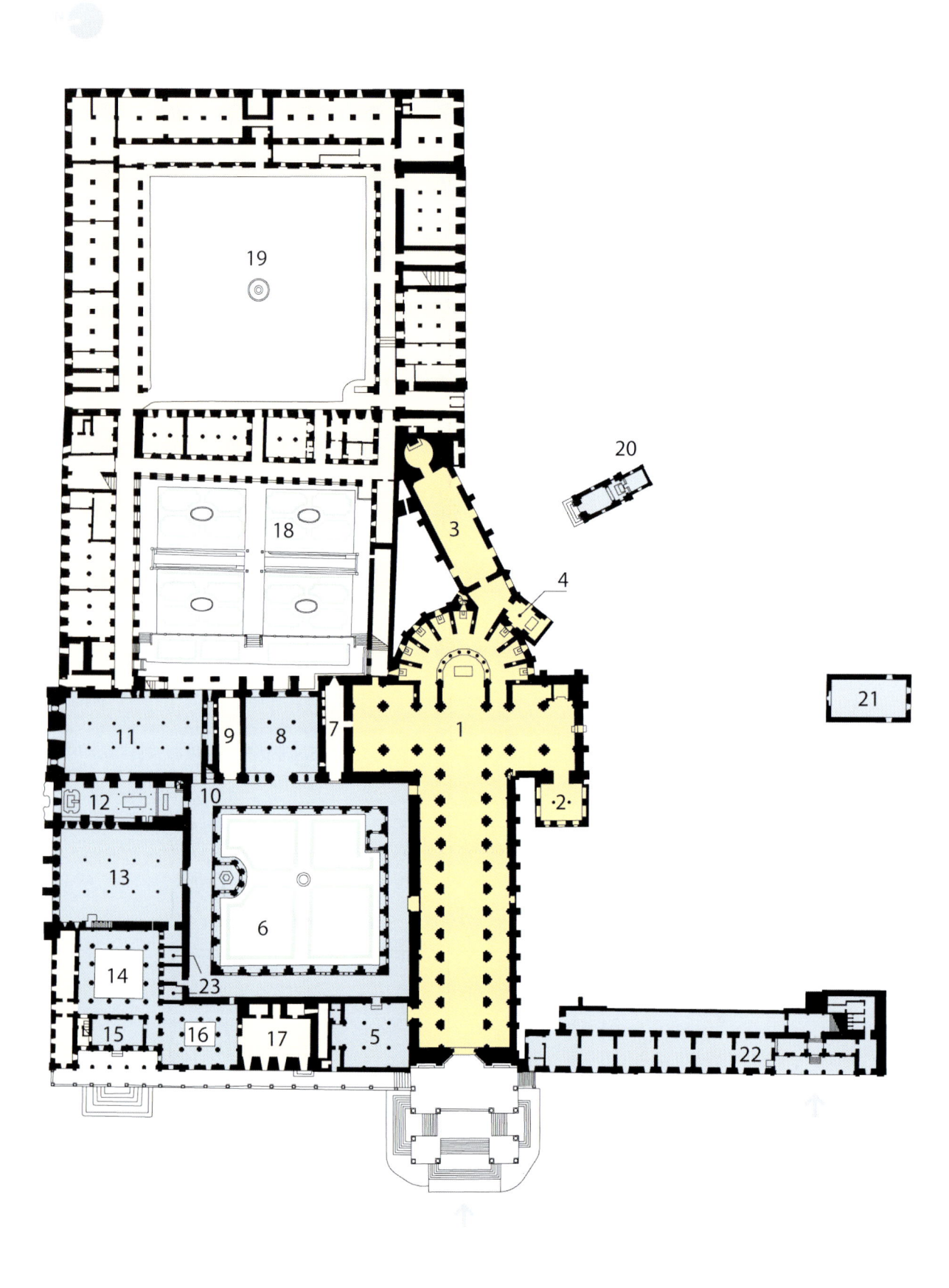

1. Church
2. Royal Pantheon
3. Manueline Sacristy *[restricted visiting]*
4. Chapel of the Lord of the Steps *[restricted visiting]*
5. Royal Hall/ Tickets
6. Cloister of Silence or of King Dinis
7. Medieval Sacristy *[not open to the public]*
8. Chapter House
9. Parlour *[shop]*
10. Access to the Dormitory *[upper floor]*
11. Monks' Hall
12. Kitchen
13. Refectory
14. Cloister of King Afonso VI
15. Entrance Lodge
16. Prison Cloister
17. Conclusion Hall *[not open to the public]*
18. Cardinal's Cloister *[not open to the public]*
19. Library Cloister or Woodcutting Cloister *[not open to the public]*
20. Chapel of Exile *[restricted visiting]*
21. Grainstore/ Multipurpose Room
22. St Bernard's Wing/ Temporary Exhibition Gallery

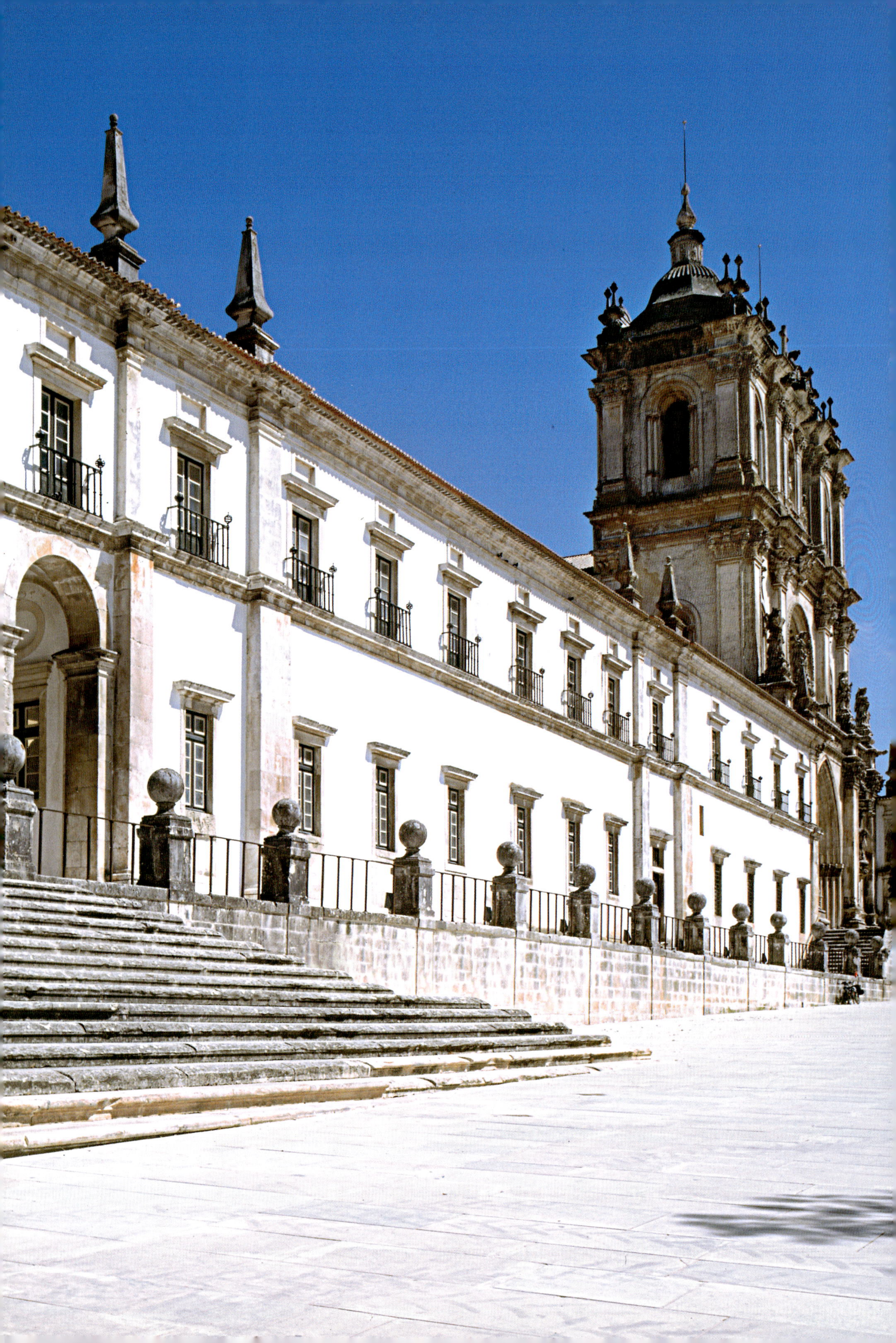

Main façade of
the monastery

THE FOUNDATION OF THE MONASTERY

The Royal Abbey of Santa Maria de Alcobaça, founded by King Afonso Henriques in the heart of the immense region of Estremadura, was one of the most important Cistercian houses in the Iberian Peninsula and, without doubt, the one most redolent with meaning – political, economic and artistic – in the territory of the emerging kingdom of Portugal.

Its foundation dates from 8 April 1153, when the Portuguese monarch granted to Bernard, Abbot of Clairvaux, the *Carta de Couto*, a charter endowing the Cistercian Order with a vast area of nearly 108,700 acres, extending from the Serra dos Candeeiros to the coast, northwards almost as far as Leiria and southwards almost to Óbidos. Until 1147, when Afonso recaptured Santarém and Lisbon from the Moors, the castles at Leiria and Óbidos had stood as outposts marking the boundaries of the Portuguese territory thus far reconquered from the invaders by Christian forces.

Despite its importance, Alcobaça was not the first institution of the White Monks (so called because of the colour of their habits) in Portugal. They had already settled in São João de Tarouca between 1143 and 1144, also in São Tiago de Sever, then later in Salzedas, where the monastery still shows traces of its long and complex history.

Over the years, various factors regarding the building of the monastery have become subjects for debate: the circumstances leading to its establishment, the site upon which it was built and the high artistic quality of its buildings, which would remain unparalleled in Portugal for decades.

The area endowed to the Order is believed by most historians to have been practically deserted, as Estremadura had been a frontier zone in the conflict between Christians and Muslims since the eighth century. The land, however, was among the most fertile anywhere in the new Christian territories, which helps to explain why the Cistercians, with their well-known agricultural leanings, decided to settle there. Having been given charge of this vast area, however, the monks were not content with merely populating it and using agricultural means to create economic prosperity there.

Immediately after their arrival, most probably following a careful evaluation of the region they were going to occupy, the monks began the construction of a building – the Old Monastery. The project was short-lived, however, and no traces of the building survive. Next came the task of organising the region economically, clearing the land, grubbing up forested areas, drying out marshland and integrating the existing population, which grew with successive waves of settlers. The exemplary development of the area into farms (or granges, as they were called), for which the Cistercians were famous, rapidly transformed the Alcobaça region into a prosperous, albeit an unstable, one.

It was under these conditions that the building of the present monastery began on 10 May 1178. The theory that it was built by monks from Tarouca is considered unlikely today. The economic, cultural and artistic conditions that prevailed in the country at that time make it highly unlikely that the monastery at Alcobaça was built by local craftsmen, in view of the fact that its church was the first building in Portugal with Gothic features.

The way work was organised among the Cistercians suggests that the new churches and abbeys were designed, and their construction supervised, by architect-monks from the mother-houses who were well schooled in the demands imposed by the Order's new, more austere, spirituality. The church of São João de Tarouca, for example, clearly takes its inspiration from Fontenay, whilst Alcobaça is modelled on the final phase of Clairvaux (Clairvaux III), from where it is likely that its master builders and a large number of its masons came. According to the legend of how the monastery at Alcobaça was founded (recounted in full in the chapter on the Hall of the Kings), Bernard of Clairvaux (later canonised as St Bernard) played a quasi-miraculous role in the recapture of Santarém, thus consolidating the sovereignty of King Afonso Henriques. The legend also recounts that five monks came from Clairvaux to establish the monastery.

Giving weight to this hypothesis is the fact that the land was donated directly to Bernard, who was a central figure in the political and cultural context of the twelfth century. Indeed, he presided over a profound re-examination of the Rule of St Benedict, which was observed throughout Christendom, advocating a return to its earliest and strictest form. This wide-ranging reform had a major effect on fundamental aspects of spirituality, as well as impacting on other factors such as artistic expression, economic organisation and even political relations.

The Cistercian Order, whose mother-house was founded in 1098 following a split with the Benedictines, was instilled, under Bernard's direction, with a sense of austerity and restraint. Deep mysticism went hand-in-hand with a neo-Platonic approach inspired by St Augustine. Indeed, it was his reading of Plato's Aesthetics that encouraged Bernard, a man of exceptional intelligence and energy, to set about changing the Cistercians' attitudes towards art. Until this time, imagery had played a crucial role in spreading the Christian message and was used extensively by the Benedictines at Cluny, who, following the teachings of Gregory the Great, championed visual images as a 'bible for the illiterate'. Under the influence of Bernard, however, Cistercian churches and monasteries were stripped of all superfluous ornamentation, including paintings, stained-glass windows and sculptures, which were deemed by St Augustine to have 'seductive' powers. As set forth in Augustine's *Exordium Cisterciensis Coenobii*, even silks and gold – chalices, reliquaries, crosses and other liturgical implements – were to be replaced by wooden crosses and by candelabra and censers made from iron. Not even the scriptoria were spared: according to Bernard's wishes, copies of psalters, missals, bibles and other codices had to be produced without recourse to the fanciful and colourful Romanesque illustration that was part of Irish, Merovingian, Carolingian and even Mozarabic tradition.

In his discussions with the abbots of Cluny and with Abbot Suger of the Royal Abbey of Saint-Denis, as well as in his *Apologia* to William of Saint-Thierry, Bernard made clear his spiritual and artistic motivations. The sense of restraint he advocated resulted in churches and monasteries of clearer structure, built according to new parameters of efficiency and an economy of resources. Decoration was reduced primarily to geometrical plant-based patterns, with plain-glass windows and a new theory of light, which although deriving from the prevailing Romanesque model, inevitably came into conflict with it.

Cistercian reforms were not, however, merely designed to promote the new concept of spirituality and dictate how art should be used in a religious context. Artistic austerity was closely linked to the new economic policy observed in the abbeys, and to the principles of efficiency that the White Monks sought to apply to every aspect of their work. Like their Cluniac brethren, Cistercian monks continued to settle in unpopulated, isolated regions where agricultural activity could flourish – conditions required, in any case, by the General Chapter of the Order of 1134. The pragmatic way they organised themselves, with the clear assignment of management tasks to the various monks of each community, meant that they avoided the problems that monasteries of other Orders encountered.

The twelfth century marked the beginning of a significant shift in the prevailing economic order of the Christian world. The growing importance of towns and trade, and subsequently of markets and paper currency, resulted in the devaluation of land ownership and feudatory rights. Conscious of this, the Cistercians avoided the mistakes made by the Cluniac monks that had led to the financial ruin of the great Monastery of Cluny around 1140.

The practices advocated by the Cistercians, and in particular by Bernard, increased the revenue of the abbeys by improving the cultivation of land and the management of resources. The granges improved farming and animal husbandry practices, and better crop rotation and fertilisation techniques were employed. New areas of land were constantly cleared and the most up-to-date farm implements were introduced. In addition, the best use was made of all available resources in a given region, in everything from the building of mills to the mining of minerals. The protection of settlers and leaseholders was another significant consideration of the Order, particularly in regions such as Alcobaça, which suffered repeated incursions by the Moors.

This pragmatic approach, along with the spiritual asceticism preached by Bernard, combined to create perfect conditions under which to maintain a system inherited from the Romanesque monastic tradition. Indeed, Bernard, whose aim it was to 'change something so that everything remained the same', stood at a transitional point: he was both the forerunner of a new era and the last representative of the old order. Thus, restraint in the use of gold and precious stones, the new rationality of the architecture, the discreet and secondary role assigned to sculpture, and the sobriety of the illuminated codices were all evidence of an economy of resources that enabled the monastic communities to keep their accounts in healthy order.

It is also important to acknowledge the significant political role played by Bernard, who, as adviser to Pope Innocent II and to the Templars, as well as preacher of the Second Crusade, was arguably the most remarkable figure of twelfth-century Europe. It was with his support that Innocent II prevailed over his rival, the antipope Anacletus II. Then, with the election in 1145 of Eugene III (a former Cistercian monk and disciple of his), Bernard's influence over the Roman Curia grew further still. However, his humility was such that he stubbornly refused any honour higher than that of abbot.

The extent of his influence was demonstrated when the *Carta de Couto* was granted directly to him by King Afonso I of Portugal, an act that proved advantageous to both parties. Afonso, who was not yet recognised as king by Rome, stood to benefit by winning the support of the most important figure of his time, while simultaneously counteracting the influence that the Cluniacs wielded among rulers in the Iberian Peninsula. For Bernard and the Cistercians it enabled the creation of a domain of extraordinary size and importance that would help consolidate their presence in the peninsula. These factors help to explain the unusual nature of the monastery at Alcobaça, both in the philosophy behind its building programme and in the dimensions of its church (106 metres long), which were the same as Clairvaux III, further suggesting that Alcobaça was directly influenced by Clairvaux. In fact, Alcobaça was the third largest among the Cistercian abbeys (after those at Vancelles and Pontigny) and was built on a scale which, until then, had been unheard of in Portugal.

The occupation of this territory by the White Monks, being the biggest monastic domain in the entire kingdom, became a vital directive in the monarch's strategy of southward expansion. Following the royal advance along the Tagus to reconquer Santarém and Lisbon, the region needed to be colonised by a population capable of creating prosperity and stability. In turn, this enabled the Cistercians to 'standardise' Christian worship in the region through the introduction of the Roman Rite. At that time the Mozarabic Rite continued to thrive among communities in Coimbra and Soure, as well as in Estremadura, as the ancient chapel of São Gião in Nazaré testifies. The Cistercian mission was, therefore, the same that had been previously undertaken by the Cluniacs in the north of the country, namely to establish the Roman Rite in order to counteract the many surviving traditions of Mozarabism, Judaism and Aryanism.

It is not surprising that Alcobaça should have been designated a 'royal' abbey, given the number of donations it received from various Portuguese monarchs, all of which played an important role in the construction of the monastic complex.

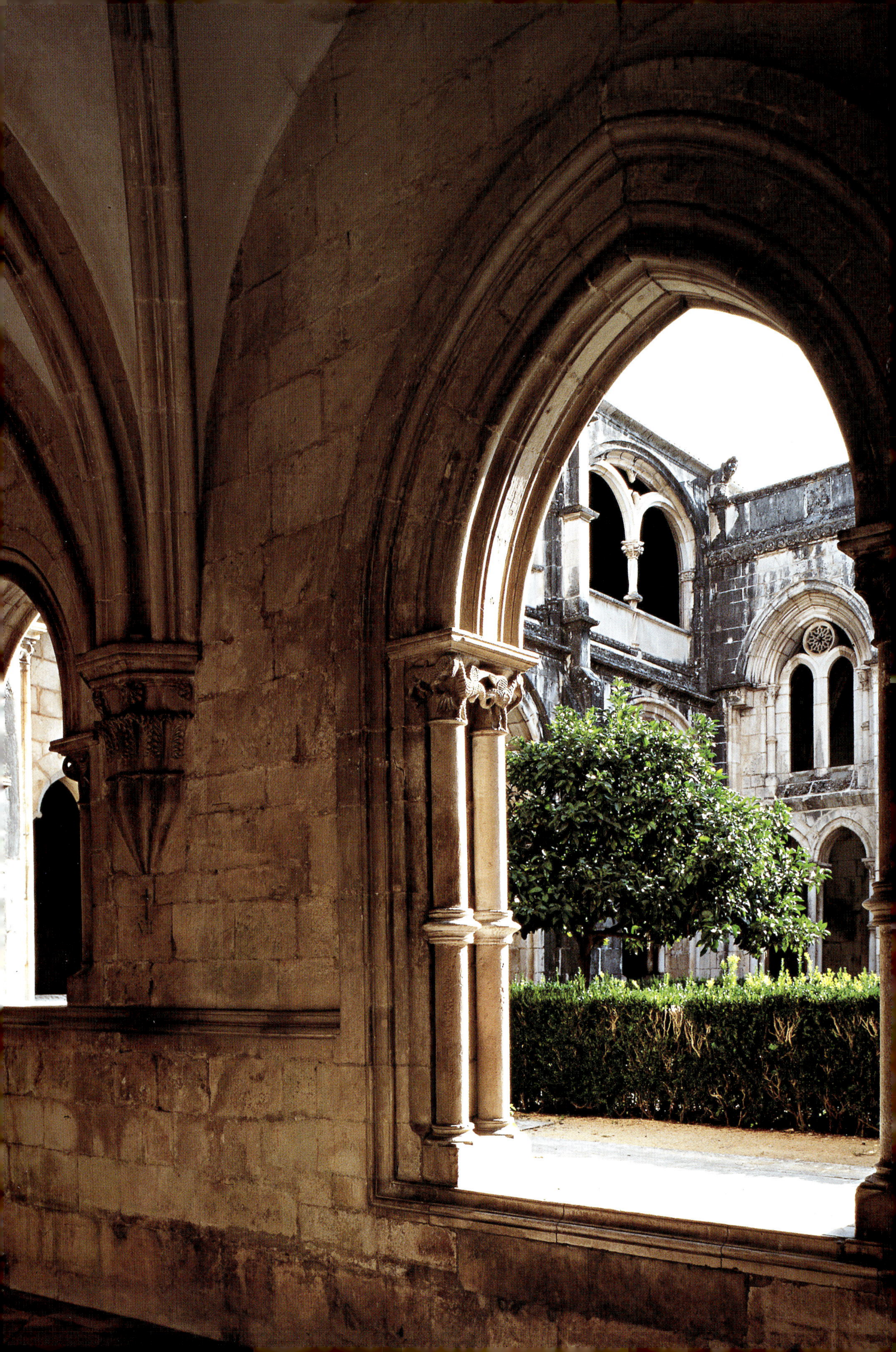

CISTERCIAN MONASTERIES IN PORTUGAL

To better understand the Cistercian presence in Portugal it is necessary to examine the way in which its monastic houses were built, and the locations they occupied around the country. Presented here is a chronological listing of the foundation of the houses of the White Monks.

São João de Tarouca, in the district of Viseu, was the first Cistercian monastery founded in the kingdom. Resulting from the transformation of a former hermitage, it was originally a Benedictine monastery, and became affiliated to the Cistercians around 1144. The transition in style from Romanesque to Gothic is clearly evident in the church, and archaeologists have recently uncovered a medieval cloister.

Affiliated to Tarouca, and dating from the same period, was São Tiago de Sever in the district of Viseu, which did not survive for long.

Santa Maria de Alcobaça followed, which was the most important of all the houses, as already mentioned.

Then came Santa Maria de Salzedas, which was founded between 1156 and 1196, and had two incarnations: the first was as the Old Monastery, which was also built on the site of a former hermitage. Work was mysteriously abandoned, however, while the church was still far from completion. Nevertheless, significant vestiges of the construction remain, particularly in the area of the chevet (or east end). Its second incarnation – as the New Monastery – situated a few hundred metres from the first one, eventually become one of the Order's leading monastic houses in Portugal. Affiliated to São João de Tarouca, it is located in the same municipality and district.

Next to emerge was the Monastery of São Cristóvão de Lafões, in the municipality of São Pedro do Sul, in the district of Viseu. Founded around 1163 and entirely renovated in 1704, the church was centrally planned in the shape of an octagon, or a rectangle with its corners cut off. It was a typical example of the Portuguese Baroque of the seventeenth and eighteenth centuries, inspired by Borromini's Roman Baroque. This was a style adopted for a number of religious buildings, two examples of which are the church of the Menino Deus in Lisbon and the church of Senhor Jesus da Piedade in Elvas.

The Monastery of Santa Maria do Bouro also resulted from the conversion of a Benedictine monastery, which had been founded on a hermitage and then 'normalised' according to the canonical principles of Rome. Cistercian since 1182 or 1195, it is located in the municipality of Amares, in the district of Braga, and has recently been converted into a hotel.

Santa Maria de Maceira Dão, in the municipality of Mangualde, in the district of Viseu, was affiliated in 1188 but underwent major reconstruction in the eighteenth century, including a remodelling of the monastic cloister. Of the eighteenth-century complex, the cloister and the remarkable church remain. The church follows the centralised plan, here taking the form of an elliptical nave joining a rectangular chancel – a design of great audacity and originality similar to that used by Nicola Nasoni in the Igreja dos Clérigos in Oporto.

Santa Maria de Fiães, in the municipality of Melgaço, in the district of Viana do Castelo is the most northerly of the Cistercian monasteries in Portugal. It is the result of the affiliation, between 1173 and 1194, of a former Benedictine monastery. Part of its Romanesque structure still remains.

Santa Maria de Seiça, at Figueira da Foz in the district of Coimbra, was donated to Alcobaça by King

Sancho I in 1195. The church was totally rebuilt in the seventeenth century. Close by stands the fascinating, centrally-planned Chapel of Nossa Senhora de Seiça, built in 1602.

Santa Maria de Aguiar, in the municipality of Castelo Rodrigo, in the district of Guarda, followed. It was founded as a Benedictine monastery on Portuguese territory, which, at a time when frontiers were constantly shifting, became part of the kingdom of Leon. The land came to Portugal at the end of the thirteenth century, at the same time as the monastery affiliated to the Cistercian Order.

The next to affiliate, also in the thirteenth century, was the Monastery of São Pedro das Águias at Tabuaço, in the district of Viseu. Its small church remains one of the gems of Portuguese Benedictine Romanesque, and its location suggests that it may also have been built on the site of an old hermitage. The affiliation of the isolated Monastery of Santa Maria de Ermelo, at Arcos de Valdevez, in the district of Viana do Castelo, also dates from the same period. An interesting peculiarity of this monastery is that its church seems initially to have been designed as a larger building, with a nave and two side aisles, but was reduced in a subsequent plan. The resulting building has a nave as well as the two arches that would have given access to apse-chapels that were never built.

The next monastic house to be affiliated, between 1200 and 1206, was the Monastery of São Mamede do Lorvão, at Penacova, in the district of Coimbra. It was the first in Portugal to be occupied by a female Cistercian monastic community. An important monastery since the Visigoth period, it became one of the leading Cluniac Benedictine houses in Portugal: it was here that the Benedictine Rule was introduced to the kingdom. Alongside those of the Augustinian Monastery of Santa Cruz in Coimbra and Santa Maria de Alcobaça, São Mamede do Lorvão had one of the most important medieval scriptoria, where important documents such as the famous medieval bestiary *Livro das Aves* and the *Apocalipse* were produced. It became affiliated to the Cistercian Order at the command of the Infanta Dona Teresa, daughter of Sancho I, who drove out the Benedictine monks and established a series of Cistercian nunneries.

At the behest of another of King Sancho I's daughters, Dona Sancha, Santa Maria de Celas was founded in Coimbra in 1215. It was the second Cistercian nunnery in Portugal.

The foundation of the Monastery of Santa Maria de Tomarães followed, in 1217. It was situated in the municipality of Tomar, in the district of Santarém, but it ceased to function at some time during the sixteenth century, and no traces of it remain.

The same fate befell the Monastery of Santa Maria da Estrela, founded in 1220. It appears never to have been completed and became defunct in 1579. It stood on the banks of the river Zêzere, in the municipality of Covilhã, in the district of Castelo Branco. It has now disappeared completely.

The Monastery of São Paulo de Frades at Coimbra, also known as the Monastery of Almaziva (indicating the presence of a Mozarabic community on the site), was founded, or more probably affiliated, in 1221.

Another of the great female Cistercian monasteries was São Pedro e São Paulo at Arouca, in the district of Aveiro. Initially founded in 716 as a 'double' community of both monks and nuns, it was dedicated to St Peter and St Paul in 951, in an early attempt to 'normalise' the house and its style of worship. It was affiliated to the Cistercian Order in 1225 through the direct intervention of the third daughter of King Sancho I, Infanta Dona Mafalda (later beatified as Santa Mafalda, the name by which the monastery is also known). Today it is one of the wealthiest monasteries in Portugal, with a vast collection of sacred art, including illuminations and medieval gold work such as the magnificently illuminated *Antiphonary* dating from the twelfth and thirteenth centuries, and the splendid French *Diptych Reliquary* (*c*. 1220) in gilded silver depicting the Annunciation, along with paintings, vestments and sculpture.

Following this was the affiliation in 1228 of a small convent of nuns, that of São Salvador de Bouças, situated on the outskirts of Oporto. Despite its relatively unremarkable history (it became defunct fairly quickly), it is considered by some historians to be one of the oldest buildings occupied by the Cistercians in Portugal.

The history of the small Monastery of Santa Maria de Júnias is rather more interesting. It was built as a Benedictine monastery in an isolated area of Gerês, but following its affiliation in 1247 it became dependent on the Cistercian Monastery of Oseira in neighbouring Galicia. Although in ruins, it retains its church and part of the cloister, which bear the influence of the Benedictine Romanesque style that spread from Braga. Santa Maria de Júnias is located in the Peneda-Gerês National Park, in a delightful rural setting in the municipality of Montalegre, in the district of Vila Real.

Another major female establishment was the Monastery of São Bento de Castris, near the town of Évora. Affiliated to the Cistercian Order in 1274, it became the most important female Cistercian monastic house in the south of the country.

Of comparable importance was the Monastery of Santa Maria de Almoster, near Santarém – also for nuns. Today it is largely in ruins, although the Gothic church still stands, as do a considerable part of the original cloister and some vestiges of the monastic buildings.

Near Lisbon, the Monastery of São Dinis e São Bernardo at Odivelas was founded between 1294 and 1305, housing a new female Cistercian monastic community. With a rather magnificent and sophisticated construction, the monastery came into existence through the patronage of King Dinis (hence the choice of patron saint) and the work of architects Antão and Afonso Domingos. The earthquake of 1755, which destroyed a large area of lower Lisbon, also caused irreparable damage to the monastery, leaving only the portal, the imposing Gothic sanctuary and part of the wings of the cloister of the great Gothic abbey church. On the eve of the expedition to Ceuta, Philippa of Lancaster died here. So too did a natural daughter of the king, whose tomb, along with that of her father, lies in the church.

Also in Lisbon is the nuns' Monastery of São Bento de Xabregas, which was founded in 1492 and was dependent on the Monastery of Alcobaça. After a few years it was transferred to the Friars of the Order of St John the Evangelist at the instigation of King Afonso V, the abbot of Alcobaça.

Another major female establishment was the Monastery of São Bernardo at Portalegre, also known as the Monastery of Nossa Senhora da Conceição. Founded in 1518 by Jorge de Melo, bishop of Guarda (a diocese, which, at the time, included the lands of the northern Alentejo) it became one of the richest Cistercian houses in Portugal, with vast artistic wealth. Some precious examples of vestments, furniture and sculpture are conserved in the Municipal Museum of Portalegre. Furthermore, Jorge de Melo, who loved the town of Portalegre and disliked Guarda (which he had perhaps never visited!), was one of the most enlightened patrons of the arts of the Portuguese Renaissance, a fact confirmed by the great altar screen, attributed to Nicholas de Chanterenne, which occupies an entire wall of the monastery church.

Of less significance was the founding of the Convent of São João de Vale Madeiro, near Canas de Senhorim, in the district of Viseu. Occupied by nuns between 1525 and 1530 near Canas de Senhorim, it became defunct in 1560.

Near Alcobaça, and wholly dependent on it for its survival, was the small Monastery of Santa Maria de Cós. Originally founded for a group of 'devout women' between 1241 and 1300, it was affiliated in 1530. It stands in the municipality of Alcobaça, in the district of Leiria.

The Monastery of São Bernardo, otherwise known as Nossa Senhora da Piedade de Tavira, was founded with a new female community at Tavira in the district of Faro in 1530, having attained some importance as the only Cistercian establishment in the Algarve.

The College of Espírito Santo – or São Bernardo – in the city of Coimbra, was founded in 1545 but was only occupied from 1549. Its foundation was part of the profound reform of the religious orders initiated by King Manuel I with the Hieronymites and continued by his successor, King João III, with the remaining orders. Its instigator was Friar Brás de Barros, and it was built in the city of Coimbra, where all the religious orders built their colleges along the Rua da Sofia (or Wisdom), towards the upper part of the city. Elevated to the category of abbey in 1596, the college later disappeared – as did many others from the same ambitious programme begun in the 1930s – in the ill-advised redevelopment of the city of Coimbra, carried out by the Estado Novo (or 'New State' regime).

The Monastery of Nossa Senhora do Desterro, founded in 1591 in the city of Lisbon, was another major Cistercian establishment. Built in an imposing style and richly decorated, it never housed a large monastic community but provided accommodation for visiting dignitaries of the Order. It was destroyed in the earthquake of 1755 but was rebuilt a short time later, in 1763, and was subsequently converted into a hospital, a function it still fulfils today as the Hospital do Desterro. The ornately decorated church, with its panels of eighteenth-century *azulejos* (painted ceramic tiles), remains.

Of lesser importance was the College of Nossa Senhora da Conceição in Alcobaça (also dependent on the Monastery of Alcobaça), established in 1648. When the building was destroyed in 1755 the college was incorporated into the buildings of the Alcobaça monastery itself, in the new south wing of the façade, until it closed.

Another minor establishment was the female Monastery of Nossa Senhora da Nazaré do Mocambo, founded in 1654 in the city of Lisbon, near Santos-o-Velho. Destroyed in the 1755 earthquake, it was rebuilt – although possibly never finished – and then subsequently disappeared.

The Monastery of Nossa Senhora da Assunção de Tabosa, at Sernancelhe, in the district of Viseu, was founded in 1685 and was the last of the Cistercian foundations in Portugal. Small in scale, it was built to house a community of nuns, and was particularly remarkable for its original architecture, with an imposing monastic façade made of granite, similar in style to the manorial houses of the period. Although a large number of the buildings remains, it is in an advanced state of ruin.

Finally, there are Portugal's two Cistercian military religious orders – the Order of Avis and the Order of Christ.

The Order of Avis first made its appearance as the Order of the Militia or of the Friars of Évora. It was created in 1176 to fight the Muslims who still occupied the territories in the south of the country. In 1211 King Afonso II endowed the Order with the lands of Avis, in the district of Portalegre, and around 1214 work began on the construction of the fortress and monastery. In 1223 the monks moved in, changing the name of the Order to Avis and establishing its headquarters there. They adopted the Rule of the Cistercian Military Order of Calatrava, founded in New Castile, Spain, and were placed under the jurisdiction of the French Cistercian abbey of Morimond. The Order became famous due to the fact that João I was its Master at the time he was proclaimed first king of the second dynasty, in 1385. It became annexed to the Portuguese Crown in 1433, and King João III secularised the Order in the sixteenth century.

The Order of Christ came about following the suppression of the Order of the Temple – or Knights Templar – on 2 May 1312. To avoid the dispersal of the Order's lands and knights, King Dinis annexed their property to the Portuguese Crown, having obtained a papal bull from Pope John XXII on 14 March 1319, authorising him to found a new Order. This Order succeeded the Templars in Portugal, taking over all their property and privileges. It was also given the Rule of Calatrava and, while dependent on Morimond, it came under the jurisdiction of Alcobaça. Its headquarters were initially established at Castro Marim but were transferred to the Templars' former mother-house, the Castle and the Convent of Christ in Tomar, in 1356. It was also secularised in the sixteenth century by King João III.

Stairs leading to the pulpit in the refectory

Cistercian Monasteries in Portugal   19

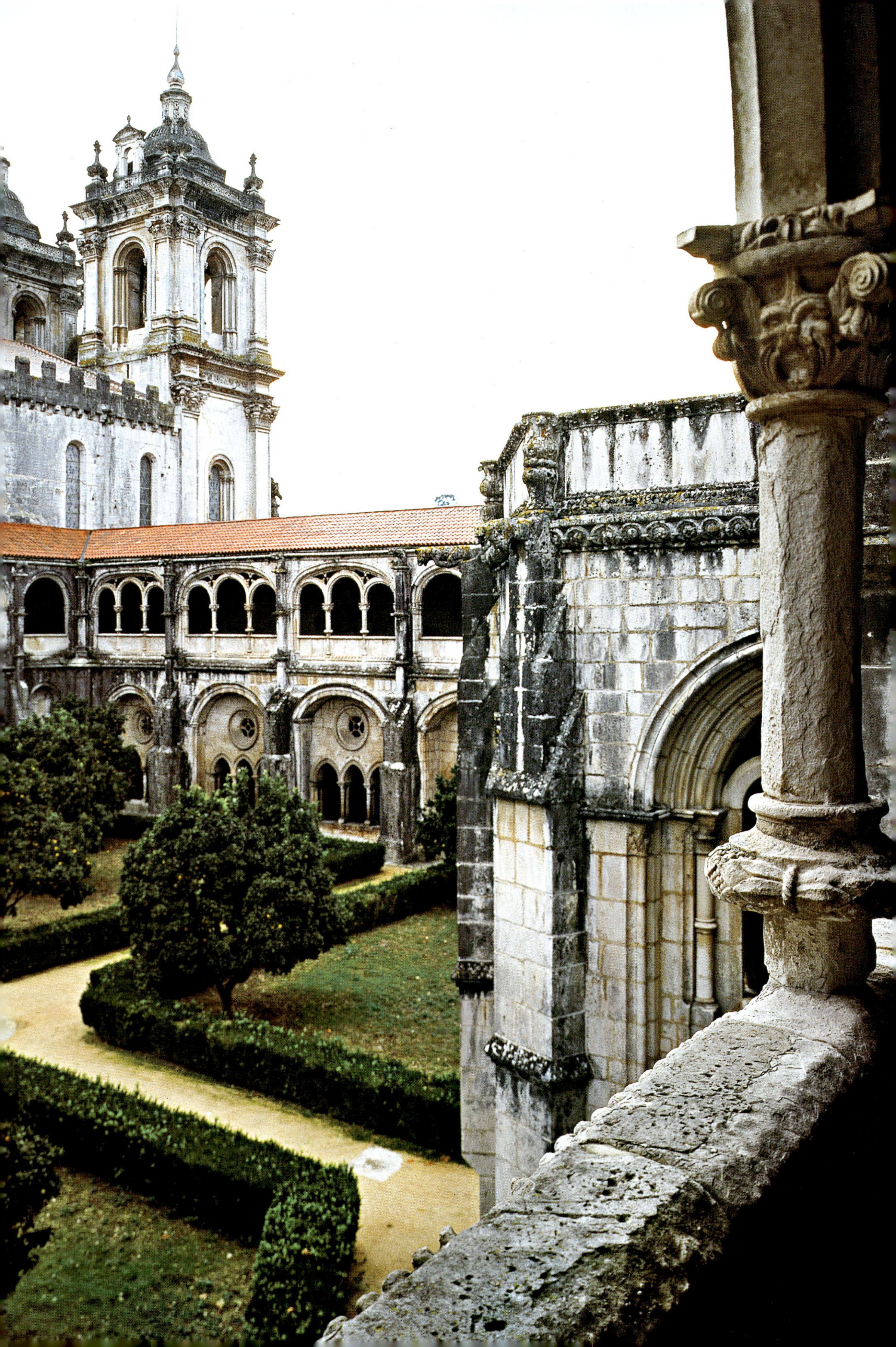

The Cloister of Silence and the north wall of the church

THE MONASTERY OF ALCOBAÇA

Until the end of the twelfth century no architectural model was to achieve such great uniformity as the Cistercian one, applied in accordance with the rules laid down in the Order's 'Charter of Charity'. These rules required that Cistercians follow the lead of the mother-house at Citeaux in France in matters of architectural design, economic affairs and religious observance. The result was the creation of a model that was emulated throughout Europe, beginning in Burgundy and spreading across France to Italy, Germany and England, and into Catalonia, Castile, Portugal and the other kingdoms of the Iberian Peninsula. In many cases it meant a complete break with the Romanesque tradition that was still predominant in religious architecture. This was particularly true of early English Gothic, in which the Cistercian influence is clearly evident.

The creation of a 'Cistercian plan' dictating the arrangement of the various buildings of the monastery was an important standardising factor that, with few and justified exceptions, remained consistent throughout Christendom. The first building of the complex was the church, which always faced east, as with earlier medieval buildings. The cloister, the heart of the monastery, was usually on the south side of the church, although at Alcobaça, for reasons of topography, it is to the north. The orientation of the church meant that it was positioned on a west-east axis, with the chancel and the presbytery facing east, that is, towards Jerusalem and the Tomb of Christ.

The various monastic outbuildings were distributed around the cloister, with the church abutting one of the wings – the south wing in the case of Alcobaça – and the remaining buildings following one another, in the eastern corridor, according to their importance. Thus, on the ground floor were the sacristy – reached through the cloister and the transept – followed by the chapter house, where the Chapter of the Order met, then the parlour and the work hall (or Monks' Hall). In the opposite corridor, to the west and usually aligned with the façade of the church, was a granary, a passageway to the church and the area that may have been the lay brothers' refectory. At Alcobaça, a medieval passageway with semicircular arches, which gives direct access to the cloister, is an interesting feature that has recently been discovered. To the south – or north in the case of Alcobaça –, on the side opposite the church, was the kitchen, situated between the lay brothers' and monks' refectories, and the calefactory, positioned between the refectory and the Monks' Hall. The external layout of this façade was in the shape of a trident, with the bodies of the two refectories and the Monks' Hall projecting beyond the kitchen and the calefactory, which was set slightly back. This arrangement was the same at both Alcobaça and Clairvaux and is clearly visible in the 1708 plan of Clairvaux by Dom Milley, a reproduction of which is in Artur Nobre de Gusmão's study of the monastery.

On the first floor of the cloister were the dormitories, with those for the monks located in the more elaborate east wing and those for the lay brothers in the west, an arrangement that reflected the differences in status between the two groups, as well as in their respective functions within the monastery: the monks were mainly involved in liturgical activities while the lay brothers' primary duties involved the maintenance of the abbey. It was an intelligent arrangement that reflected the practical sense of the Cistercians.

The choice of site for a new monastery was always based on two important criteria: the land had to be more or less level, and a spring or stream should be close by. At Alcobaça, the presence of two nearby rivers made it possible to devise a scheme that both supplied the abbey with water and provided a system for waste disposal, thus ensuring the smooth operation of the dormitory latrines, an important factor in the Cistercian principles of hygiene. The large *levada* (or watercourse) that brought water to the monastic complex is still there today, traversing it from south to north and passing beneath the new sacristy and through the cultivated land in the monastery precincts. Today, this area is occupied by the Cloister of the Cardinal (also known as the Novices' Cloister), one of the seventeenth-century additions.

The building work at Alcobaça would have progressed rather slowly, given the military and economic difficulties of the time. The major Moorish attack of 1195, which forced the monks to flee and caused damage to the works, presented a serious setback. Only after the reorganisation of the territory and of the monastery itself could work be resumed. It is assumed that by 1223 work would have been sufficiently advanced to allow the monks to move into the New Abbey. It was only completed, however, in 1252, when the church was finally consecrated. Artur Nobre de Gusmão argues that the date of the move into the New Abbey appears to contradict surviving evidence: it is known that the church was a long way from completion at the end of the first quarter of the thirteenth century but it can be assumed that if the monks did indeed move in, at least the dormitories, kitchen and refectory must have been completed – a fact which is very difficult to prove. Add to this the various problems that arose with the construction of the main cloister, which was not built until the reign of King Dinis (at least in its present form), and there is much room for speculation.

The *levada*, crossing the Cardinal's Cloister

Inscription on the north interior wall of the church indicating the position of the *aqueductus*

Inscription on the Reading Cloister, next to the church doorway, alluding to the transfer of the monastic community to the 'new abbey'

The Monastery of Alcobaça 23

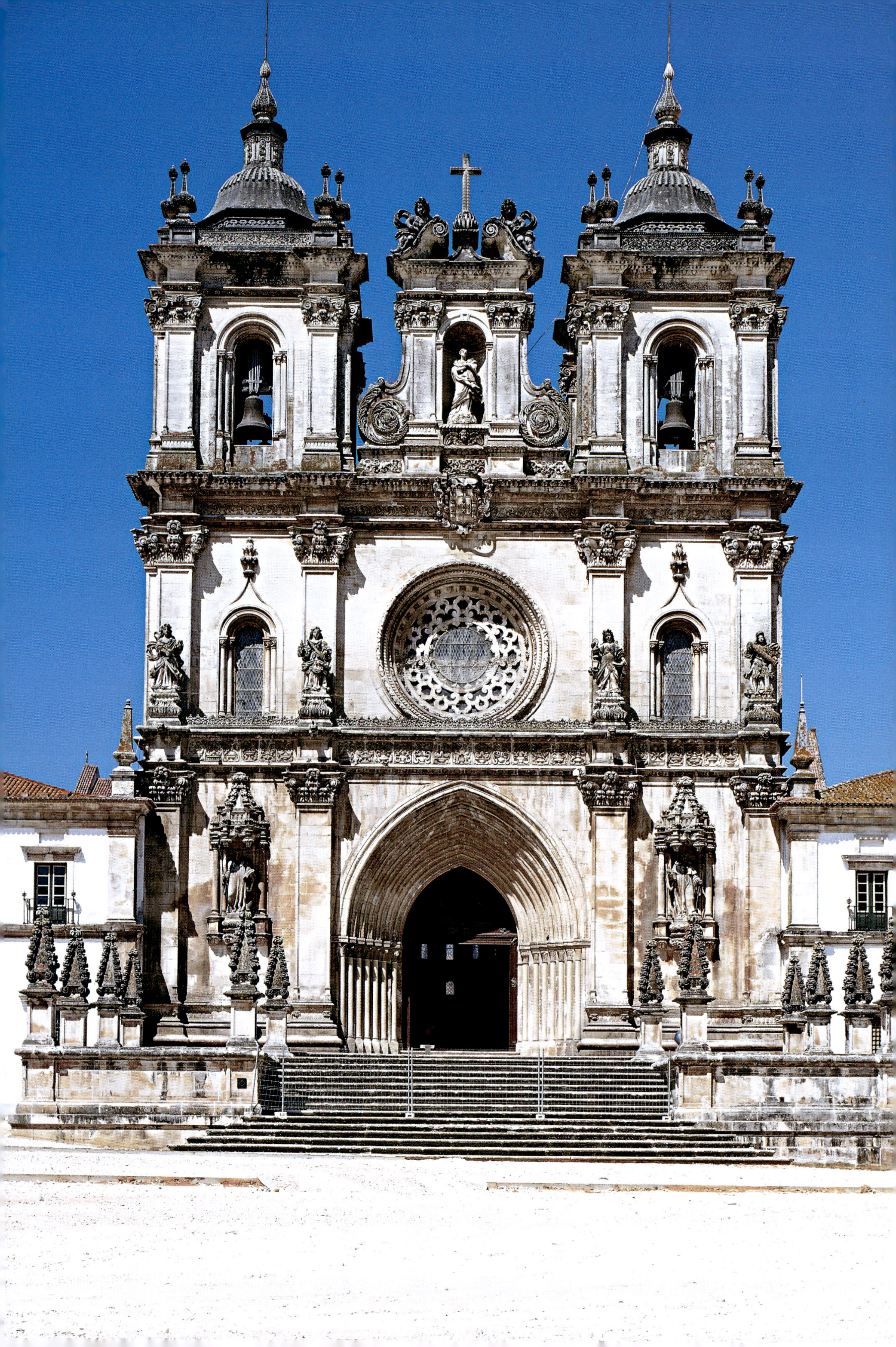

Church façade

THE CHURCH

More than any other building of this architectural complex, the church of Alcobaça has provoked an intense and passionate debate. The main protagonists are a Cistercian monk, Dom Maur Cocheril, who spent his life studying the history and artistic elements of the Order, and the great Portuguese specialist on Cistercian art, Professor Artur Nobre de Gusmão. The main difference of opinion between these two experts relates to the various phases of construction of the church, and it is only through archaeological analysis of the methods employed, and a study of the stonemason's marks or 'initials' – something that is already underway – that this can be resolved.

It certainly appears that the construction of the church at Alcobaça began, as was common in the Middle Ages, and particularly among the Cistercians, with the chevet (or east end). The chancel would have been built first, followed by the transept and crossing and, finally, the main body of the church, with its nave and two side aisles. Consecration of the church may not have been carried out until the building was complete but it is possible that it took place once solely those parts essential for the celebration of the Eucharist were finished: the ambulatory, chancel, presbytery, and the transept and crossing areas. In this case, the remaining sections of the building may have been only partially built by the year of the church's consecration, 1252. This would not have been unusual for a project of this scope and size, and it would help to explain some of the apparent anomalies that exist with regards to the construction process.

It is not known with any certainty when the imposing church façade was completed. The original has not survived but it is thought to have followed the Cistercian tradition of having a triangular pediment, as at Fontenay or San Galgano. The present façade, completed in 1725 to Friar João Turriano's plans, follows the Baroque model, with two towers and a central section. This was also adopted at Santa Maria do Bouro, Nossa Senhora da Abadia, Seiça and Salzedas. What remains of the original is more or less limited to the lower level of the façade, into which the deep pointed portal opens, framed by seven pairs of colonnettes with delicate capitals decorated by plant designs. Two niches housing the eighteenth-century statues of St Bernard and St Benedict were added later. The intermediate level of the façade, separated from the lower one by a frieze of classical motifs, still has a rose window at its centre (its original location), although it has been totally redesigned and rebuilt. To the side, above the frieze, are four more Baroque statues representing the four cardinal virtues: Fortitude, Prudence, Justice and Temperance. On the upper floor is the central section flanked by two towers topped with urns and pinnacles, and surmounted by the Cross. Here, the image of the Virgin as Our Lady of the Assumption is safeguarded in a niche, in a clearly Cistercian and Bernadine invocation, since it was St Bernard who placed the Cistercian abbeys under the protection of the Virgin.

As at Clairvaux, a wide narthex (or porch) would have stood in front of the façade. The single flight of steps leading up to the narthex was restored during later renovation work. There are examples of this particular part of a church surviving to the present day, for instance at Poblet in Spain. The narthex probably had a funerary function, in the tradition of many Romanesque buildings, since the Chapter of the Order prohibited burials within churches. This followed the tradition begun at the abbey church of Citeaux itself, where the White Monks had attained such prestige that they adapted the narthex to house the tombs of the Dukes of Burgundy, and it came to serve as their pantheon. This is not dissimilar to what happened in Portugal.

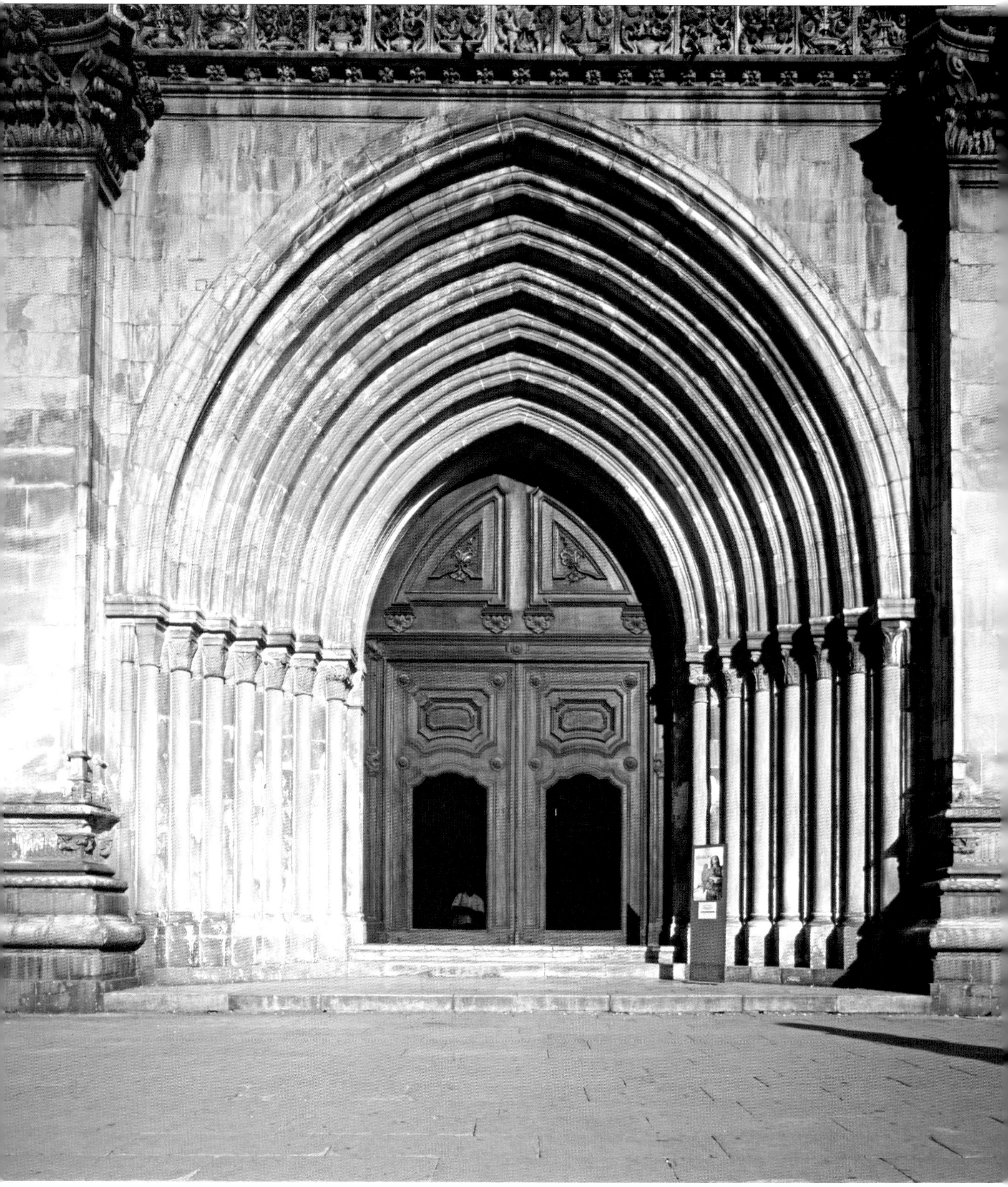

Main entrance to the church

Lateral view of the tomb of Inês de Castro, depicting stages in the life of Christ

Lateral view of the tomb of Pedro I, depicting stages in the life of St Bartholomew, his patron saint

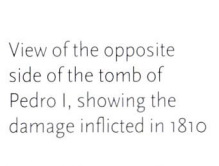

View of the opposite side of the tomb of Pedro I, showing the damage inflicted in 1810

View of the opposite side of the tomb of Inês de Castro, showing the damage inflicted by Napoleon's troops

    The funerary function fulfilled by the narthex was transferred to the adjacent pantheon in the eighteenth century. The only exceptions were the impressive tombs of King Pedro I and Queen Inês de Castro, extraordinary works of art in the panoply of fourteenth-century European funerary sculpture, which were placed in the transept. They were commissioned by King Pedro himself after the tragic death of his beloved in 1355. She was laid to rest there on 2 April 1361, followed later by the king himself on 25 January 1367. Placed in the south arm of the transept, the tombs suffered a number of vicissitudes during their existence, starting in 1569 when King Sebastião, critical of King Pedro's illicit affair, ordered the tombs to be opened. In 1810 the French soldiers of Napoleon destroyed the mummified bodies of the king and his lover, and irrevocably damaged the tombs. In the eighteenth century they were relocated to the new pantheon, and were only returned to the transept in 1956, the tomb of King Pedro being placed in the south arm and that of Queen Inês's in the north.

    The detailed sculpture on the tombs approaches that of the finest French Gothic, and they are unique in Portugal in both iconographic and sculptural terms. The recumbent statues, sculpted in high relief upon the lids, follow the tradition of the period. They depict a bearded King Pedro as a knight holding a sword, surrounded by angels and with a powerful mastiff – a symbol of loyalty and protection – at his feet. The statue of Inês de Castro, her rich vestments and facial features more delicately rendered, shows her with an elaborate canopy over her head and a small pet dog asleep at her feet. Beneath the ornate flowered arcades, the sides of the tombs depict two major Christian themes, in addition to passages from the lives of Christ and St Bartholomew. King Pedro's shows the Wheel of Fortune, evoking the Myth of Origins, while that of Queen Inês portrays the Final Judgement, with Calvary shown in counterpoint at the head. Finally, belief in the Resurrection and Eternal Life – the alpha and omega of the Christian timeline

28   The Monastery of Alcobaça

The south transept, with the tomb of Pedro I, showing the rose window and large side windows that give it light

The north transept, with the tomb of Inês de Castro, showing the door leading to the Monks' Dormitory via the Matins Staircase (*Escada das Matinas*)

The tomb of Inês de Castro, showing the baldachin that overhangs it

The tomb of Pedro I, with the mastiff lying at his feet

The head of the tomb of Inês de Castro: Calvary

The head of the tomb of King Pedro I: The Wheel of Fortune

The foot of the tomb of Inês de Castro: The Final Judgement

The foot of the tomb of Pedro I: The Good Death of the King, accompanied by Cistercian monks

30   The Monastery of Alcobaça

– is explicit in the inscription 'A: E: AFIN: DOMUDO' on the king's tomb, meaning: 'The beginning and the end of the world' (as interpreted by Maria José Goulão and Francisco Pato Macedo), or 'Here is the end of the world' (according to José Custódio Vieira da Silva).

On entering the church one is struck by the grandiosity and purity of the austere interior. Its huge dimensions and verticality suit the plain lines of the architecture and sculpture, which is in local white limestone. This is the largest church in Portugal and one of the most vertical, comparable only to Santa Maria da Vitória at Batalha or Santa Maria da Flor da Rosa near Crato, both of which date from the fourteenth century. What is extraordinary in this great church of three aisles is that the central nave and narrow side aisles are of equal height, which goes against the 2:1 rule of proportion that prevailed in the

General view, towards the east of the central nave

The north aisle, to the east

Order. This was an indication that Alcobaça, with its beautifully executed vaulted roof, was special among the Cistercian abbeys.

The church has a Latin cross plan, with the three aisles making up the main body, a complex transept (as Pedro Dias points out) with two aisles, and a chevet, with the presbytery surrounded by a broad ambulatory, as at Clairvaux III or Oseira. This type of design was also a tradition of the great Romanesque pilgrimage abbey churches along the route to Santiago de Compostela, for instance at the Cathedral of Santiago and the churches of Saint-Sernin in Toulouse or Sainte-Foy in Conques. The influence of the great Romanesque monuments of Burgundy, the region central to the genesis of the Order, is also evident in the architectural solutions and proportions that were adopted for the chevets of its churches.

The building would have been lit by the rose window and two large windows on either side of it on the façade, but additional lighting would have come from tall narrow openings in the side walls of the main body of the church, and also from the windows at both ends of the transept and those in the chevet. The chevet is unique in that it is supported by the first Gothic flying buttresses to be built in Portugal, which were propped against, as opposed to set into, the structure that was to be sustained. The rest of the church is supported by buttresses, which, in the south wall of the aisles and at the end of the south transept, correspond to the line of the transverse arches and colonnades respectively. The north transept led directly to the monastic buildings and the lighting here is more subtle, provided by just a small quatrefoil rose window that opens above the roofs of the Monks' Dormitory. Below, there would have been two doors, one that opened onto the medieval sacristy, which no longer occupies its original position

The transept, showing the division into two aisles

The narrowest aisle in the transept

34 The Monastery of Alcobaça

The Church 35

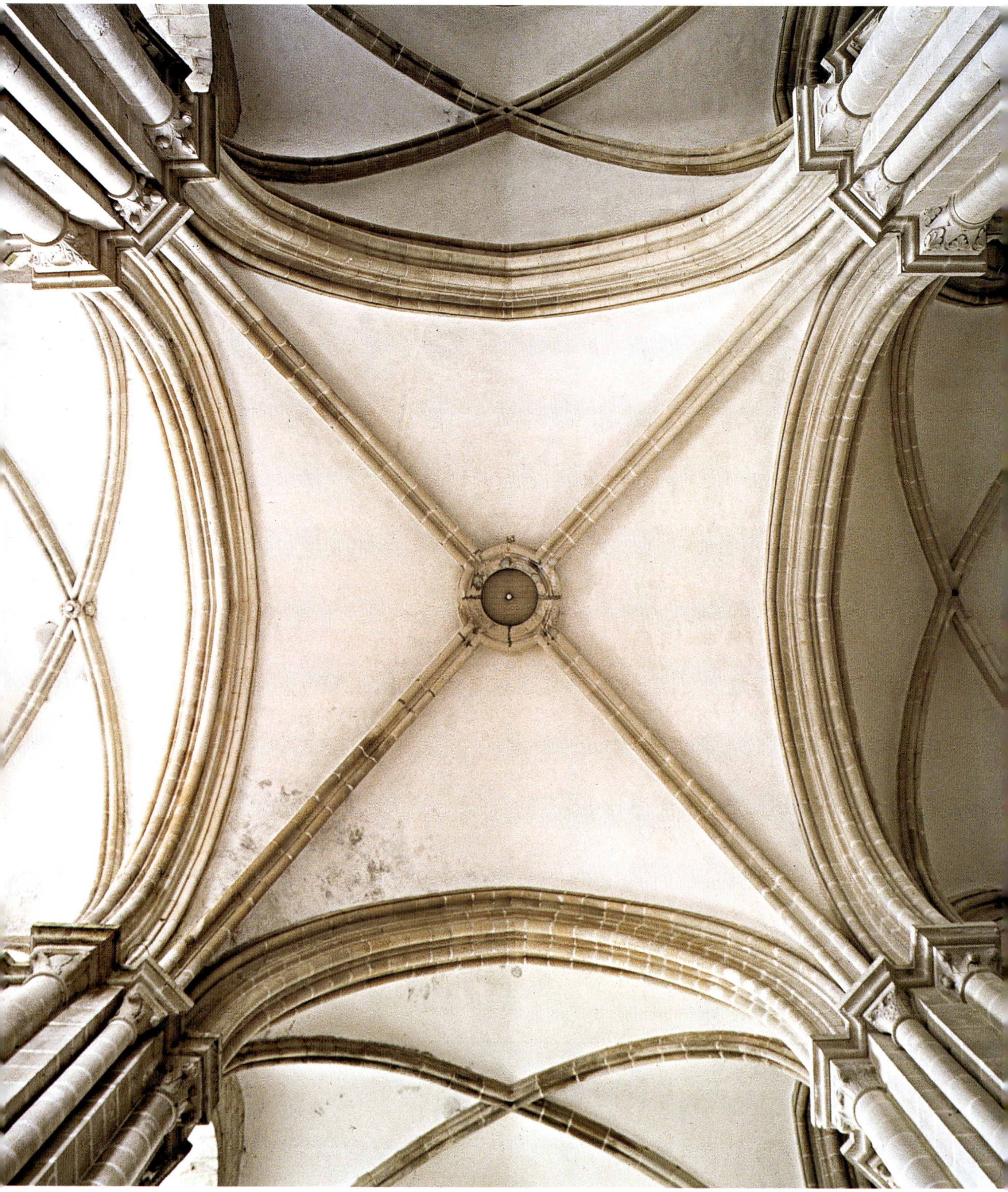

Vaulted ceilings above the crossing, showing the springing of the ribs above the central nave, transept and chancel

but which is visible in the surface of the walls; the other opened onto the dormitory, allowing the monks direct access to the church via the Matins Staircase (*Escada das Matinas*). The dormitory door is no longer there but it was undoubtedly of a similar design to that used at Fontenay, where it was elevated in relation to floor level.

At the opposite end of the same transept, beneath the rose window and the two large windows, the small door leading to the monks' cemetery still exists. On the north side of the wall of the main body of the church there are no buttresses. Maur Cocheril maintains that this is due to the need for the main cloister to be built against this wall, with the support of the structure being provided simply by making

The central nave, to the west, showing the rose window in the façade

The Church 37

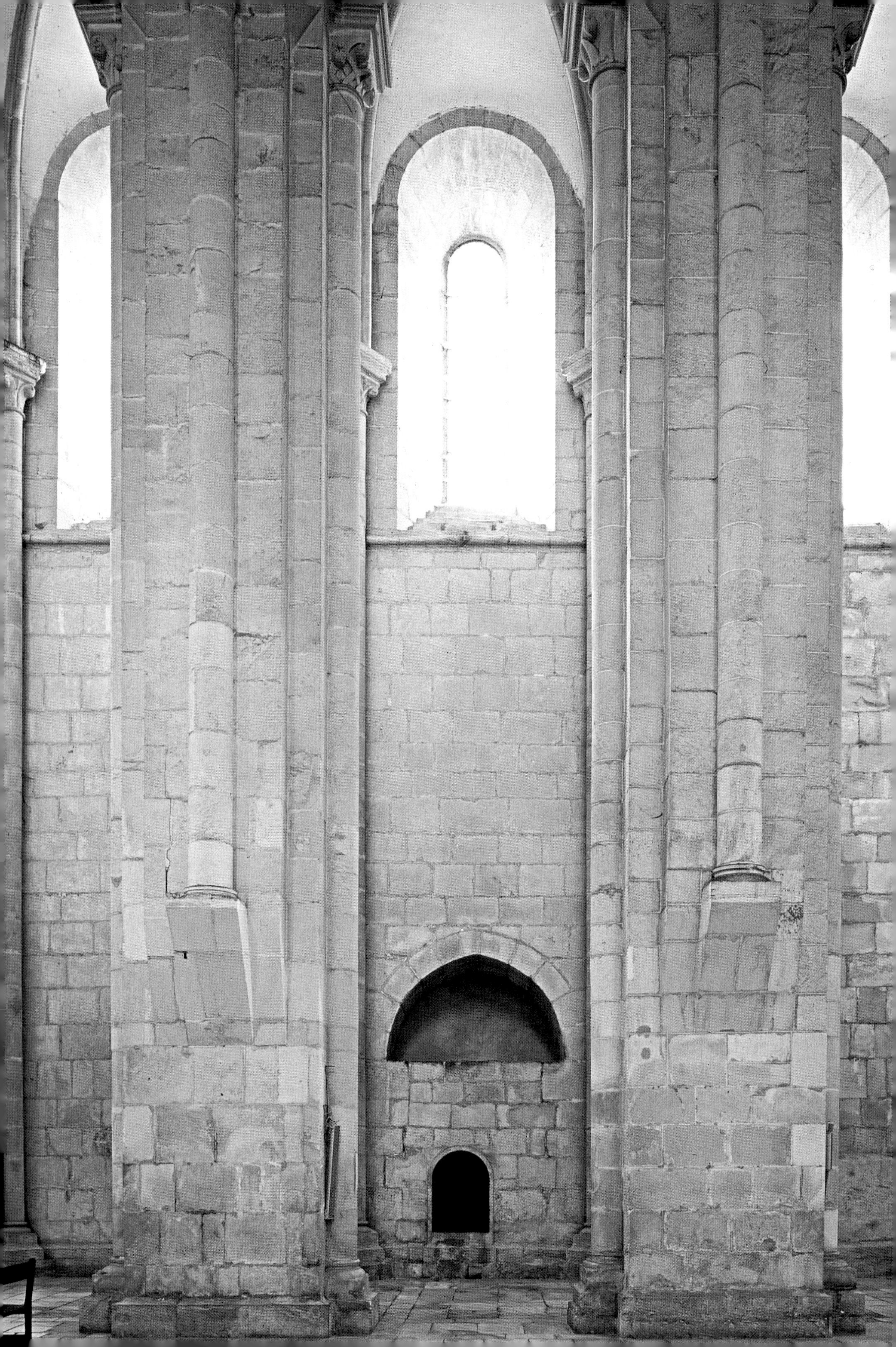

Transversal view, with the pillars and window slits in the south wall

General view of the transept, showing the tomb of Inês de Castro, the rose window in the background and the large windows high up on the south side

Buttresses outside the apse

The Church 39

Doorway leading to the Matins Staircase (*Escada das Matinas*) from the dormitory

the walls thicker. This is difficult to determine from the available plans, although Cocheril has managed to measure an additional 70cm thickness in this wall. While this question is not entirely settled from a structural point of view (one might wonder why the monks would place inelegant buttresses on the outside of the south wall if it were possible to avoid them), Cocheril's explanation seems valid when considering other elements of the construction of the cloister. On the outside, according to Gusmão, the battlements or merlons that crown the entire building (a feature common to many Romanesque churches) indicated that the abbey was the last bastion of an area that was still militarily unstable. Cocheril, however, plays down the significance of these structural elements, seeing them as decorative features that could be interpreted as 'a rhetorical show of strength'.

The configuration of a presbytery surrounded by an ambulatory closely follows the Romanesque pattern, a striking example of which can be seen at Conques, and one that is repeated in many Cistercian churches, including Clairvaux III. It was brought to Alcobaça by the architect-monk responsible for its design, believed to be a certain Didier or Desidério, although this has not been proved. The arrangement

The highest point of the transept, to the south

South wall of the church, showing the succession of buttresses supporting it

The Church 41

is very much in line with the traditions of Romanesque architecture in Burgundy and the rest of France, especially those of Burgundian Cistercian architecture, notably evident at Clairvaux III, which was completed around 1185.

This seems to support Gusmão's theory that it is unlikely that the construction plans would have been changed in such a short space of time. It also contradicts Cocheril's hypothesis that there might have been an Alcobaça I and an Alcobaça II. If this were true, the Alcobaça building would initially have been modelled on Fontenay, although shorter in length and with a square east end and four rectangular apse-chapels, again following the original plan for Clairvaux. Based simply on chronology, this supposition increases the likelihood that monks from São João de Tarouca were involved. If plans had indeed been changed, this would have happened after the building was partly destroyed in an attack by the Moors in 1195.

This theory is flawed for a number of reasons, not least because of the important role played by Bernard in establishing the monastery. Firstly, rules laid down by the General Chapter of the Cistercian Order required each new abbey to be occupied by an abbot and 12 monks, and it is unlikely that they would have come from the recently founded house at Tarouca. Furthermore, the plan finally implemented at Alcobaça only

North wall of the church, from the side of the Cloister of Silence

General view of the crossing and chancel

The Church 43

got underway in 1178, when work on Clairvaux III was already fairly well advanced. It would not have made sense for Clairvaux's Portuguese sister-house to follow a plan that the monks there already considered obsolete. It is also improbable that over such a short period – and with the limited resources available – they would have abandoned a church project already underway – one of very similar dimensions to the present one – and adopted a new plan simply because it was more architecturally up-to-date.

It remains relevant, however, to consider some of the other issues concerning the construction of the church. One of these concerns the innovativeness of the designs, even when they are integrated into apparently conservative structures. This is the case with the elevation of the chancel, which occurs on three levels. The first, at ground level, is separated from the ambulatory by a set of stout columns topped by plant-decorated capitals with voluminous crockets, from which stilted and pointed arches spring. The intermediate plane is less decorative and has three small openings. The upper one is larger, with tall windows providing the main source of light in the chevet.

The ambulatory also follows the model of Clairvaux III, with nine radiating trapezoid-plan chapels roofed by tunnel vaults and arranged around the semicircle. The sixth chapel on the left was removed to give access to the new or Manueline sacristy, an eighteenth-century rebuilding of the imposing construction commissioned by King Manuel I in the early sixteenth century. This occurred as a result of the new requirements of the liturgical rite, which were no longer met by the small medieval space. The atrium, roofed by a typically Manueline, almost flat vault, has survived from the sixteenth century, as has the original door in which mouldings on the side and on the arch resemble a knotty and blossoming tree surmounted by a shield showing the Royal Coat of Arms. It is similar to the one on the opposite Chapel of the Senhor dos Passos, commissioned to be rebuilt by Friar Manuel de Barbosa in 1756. All this is the work of João de Castilho, who was also responsible for the design of the new sacristy after the original was destroyed by the earthquake of 1755. It is remarkable for its decoration of stuccos and ceiling paintings, particularly a magnificent Apotheosis of St Bernard, a distinctly Baroque work from around 1770, as well as the large chests and other surviving furniture from the time of João V.

At the end of the new sacristy is one of the most extraordinary rooms of the entire complex, the Reliquary Chapel (*Capela das Reliquias*). Built between 1669 and 1672, during the period when Friar

North entrance of the ambulatory

The chancel and ambulatory

Lower part of the chancel

44   The Monastery of Alcobaça

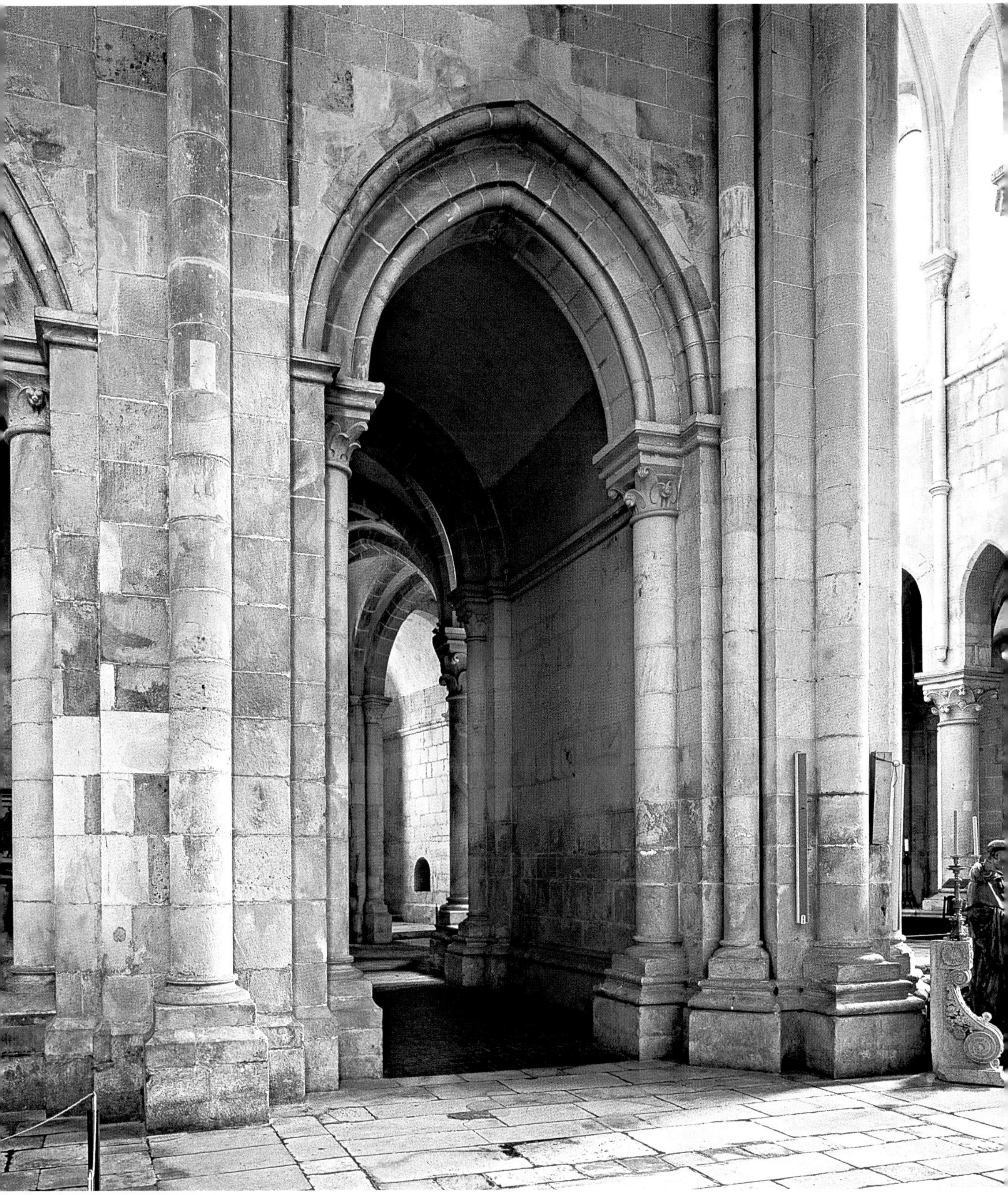

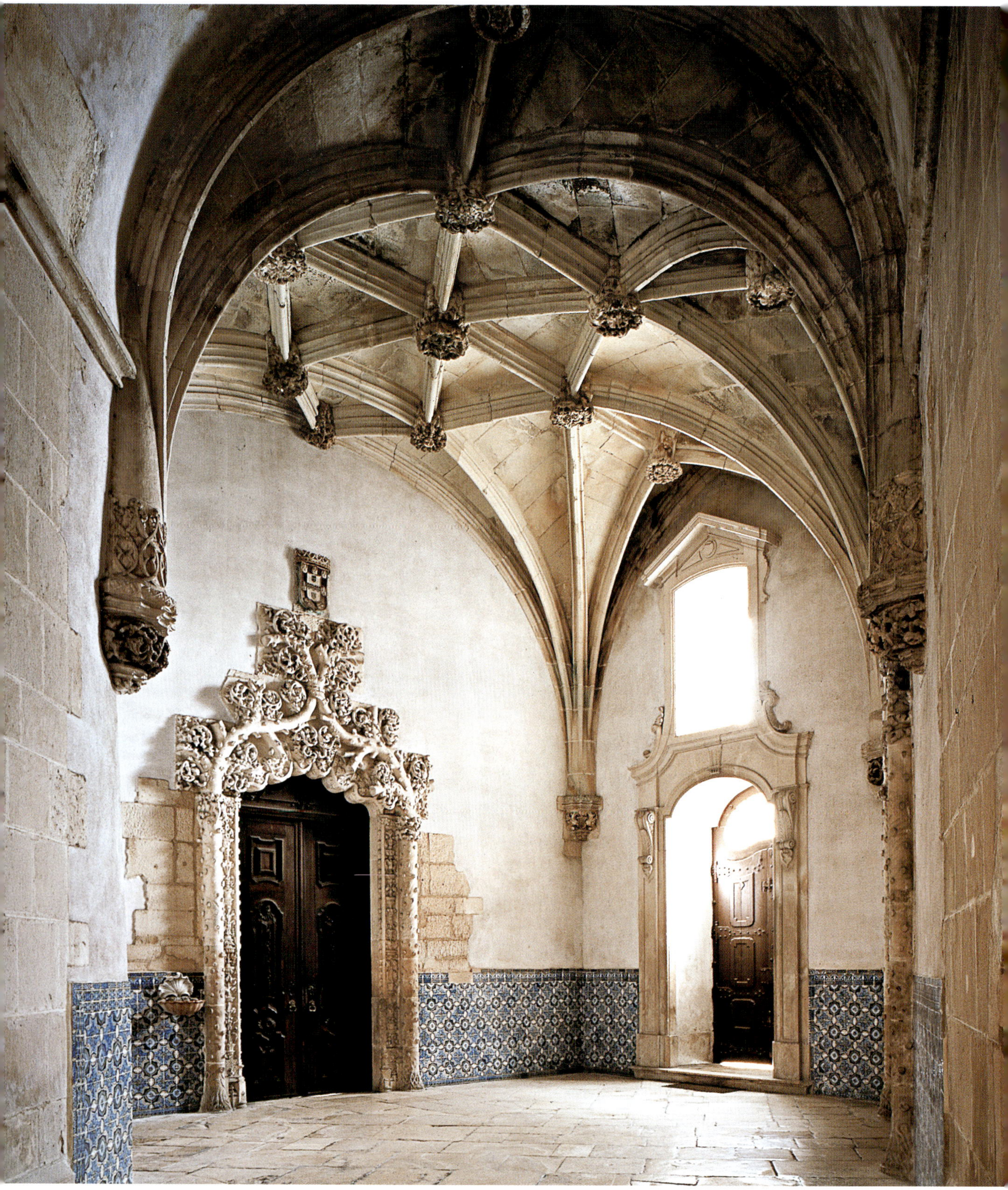

Atrium leading to
the new sacristy

Doorway leading
to the new sacristy

Fresco painted on
the ceiling of the new
sacristy: Apotheosis
of St Bernard

The Church 47

Constantino de Sampaio was abbot, it is a small, centrally planned polygonal room lit by a central lantern. Lined with polychrome and gilded wood, the niches along its walls house seven statues and 71 reliquary busts made of wood and polychrome terracotta. The circular framework of gilded wood entirely covers the octagonal wall up to the base of the dome in the stone roof. The reliquaries are divided into three types: full-length statues featuring the Virgin, a dominant figure in Cistercian imagery, in the centre; the reliquary busts of varying dimensions and typology along the six levels into which the structure is divided; and a smaller number of reliquary arms which would have been displayed alongside goldware and hangings.

The vaulted roofs of the church's three aisles are supported by crossed ribs culminating in small bosses. The ribs spring from bevelled corbels located at the angle formed between the plant-decorated capitals from which the transverse arches and wall-ribs start, both of them pointed and with finely executed

The Reliquary Chapel
(*Capela das Relíquias*)

profiles. This set of supporting structures stands on large piers with a flat intrados. In the central nave these famous Cistercian wall piers, with their engaged half-columns, project from bevelled corbels a third of the way up.

The differing styles of these piers have also given rise to debate and have been used to support the theory that the church was built in three separate phases. Beginning at the transept, the first four bays, with their cruciform piers and floral decoration on the corbels, seem to belong to an initial period of construction. The next six bays, with their half-columns engaged in stouter piers and long, oblique, rectangular corbels, appear to belong to the second phase. The last two bays next to the façade, where the corbels have a more complex profile and end in cyma mouldings, would correspond to the third phase.

Each of these spaces served a different and well-defined function. The first four bays, in addition to the two in the transept, provided a space for the monks' choir, accessible either through the dormitory

Detail of the capitals, arches and ribs in the crossing

Detail of a supporting arch in the south aisle

Detail of a formeret between the central and north aisles

The Church 49

Corbel with floral decoration in the central nave

Rectilinear corbel in the central nave

Detail of corbel in the central nave

via the north arm of the transept or through the door which led to the east wing of the cloister, or the chapter wing. It is important to remember that the various spaces within a Cistercian abbey had a strict hierarchy that was rigorously respected and, in the early days, the abbeys were not open to lay believers. Furthermore, the monks and lay brothers had to keep to their own areas and passageways. This explains why the next six bays were assigned to the lay brothers' choir, accessed in the medieval period from their corridor through the door in the north wall of the church, between the first and second piers. This door presently gives access to the Hall of the Kings and to the Choir of the Sick, which was positioned before the atrium (an assembly space that took up the two bays immediately after the façade).

While the differing styles of these columns, and particularly of their corbels, seem to support the hypothesis that they were built at different times, they also serve to underline how architecture and decoration was used in Cistercian monasteries to reinforce the distinction between monks and lay brothers. While it has been established that the construction of the medieval monastery continued over an extremely long period (the church alone took almost a century), it is noticeable how the varied shapes of the piers and corbels, and the different styles of decoration, are harmonised by a greater unity in the capitals supporting the arcades. This suggests that at every stage the plans for the construction of the building always intended to use architectural detail to reflect the hierarchical nature of the Cistercian community.

In addition to the aforementioned chapels in the ambulatory, others existed beneath the choirs, as well as four others that opened into the east wall of both arms of the transept. This arrangement constituted an essential ecclesiastical structure, in line with the Cistercian precept of holding mass only once a day in each chapel. Although this practice was abandoned, it was resumed in the seventeenth and eighteenth centuries in an attempt to bring the church up-to-date both artistically and spiritually.

Scenes and images in carved wood and terracotta, most of which have not survived, were then conceived to fill the former spaces of the medieval liturgy with new and complex symbolism and imagery. The Chapel of the Death of St Bernard, in the south arm of the transept, is remarkable for a fine work by the terracotta sculptors of Alcobaça. Begun around 1687 to 1690, and completed between 1702 and 1705, when Friar Pedro of Lancaster was abbot, it was badly damaged by French soldiers and by humidity in the nineteenth century. It then underwent careful restoration, with part of its original polychrome work being recovered, although it was not possible to reconstruct it in its entirety. According to Cocheril this was partly due to the fact that it had already been impaired by an unfortunate restoration carried out by the monks at the beginning of the nineteenth century.

Church capitals decorated with stylised plant motifs

Church capitals decorated with plant motifs with voluminous crockets

Church capital decorated with plant motifs

The Church 51

Chapels in the south wing of the transept, showing the tomb of Pedro I

Chapel showing the Death of St Bernard group

The Death of
St Bernard group

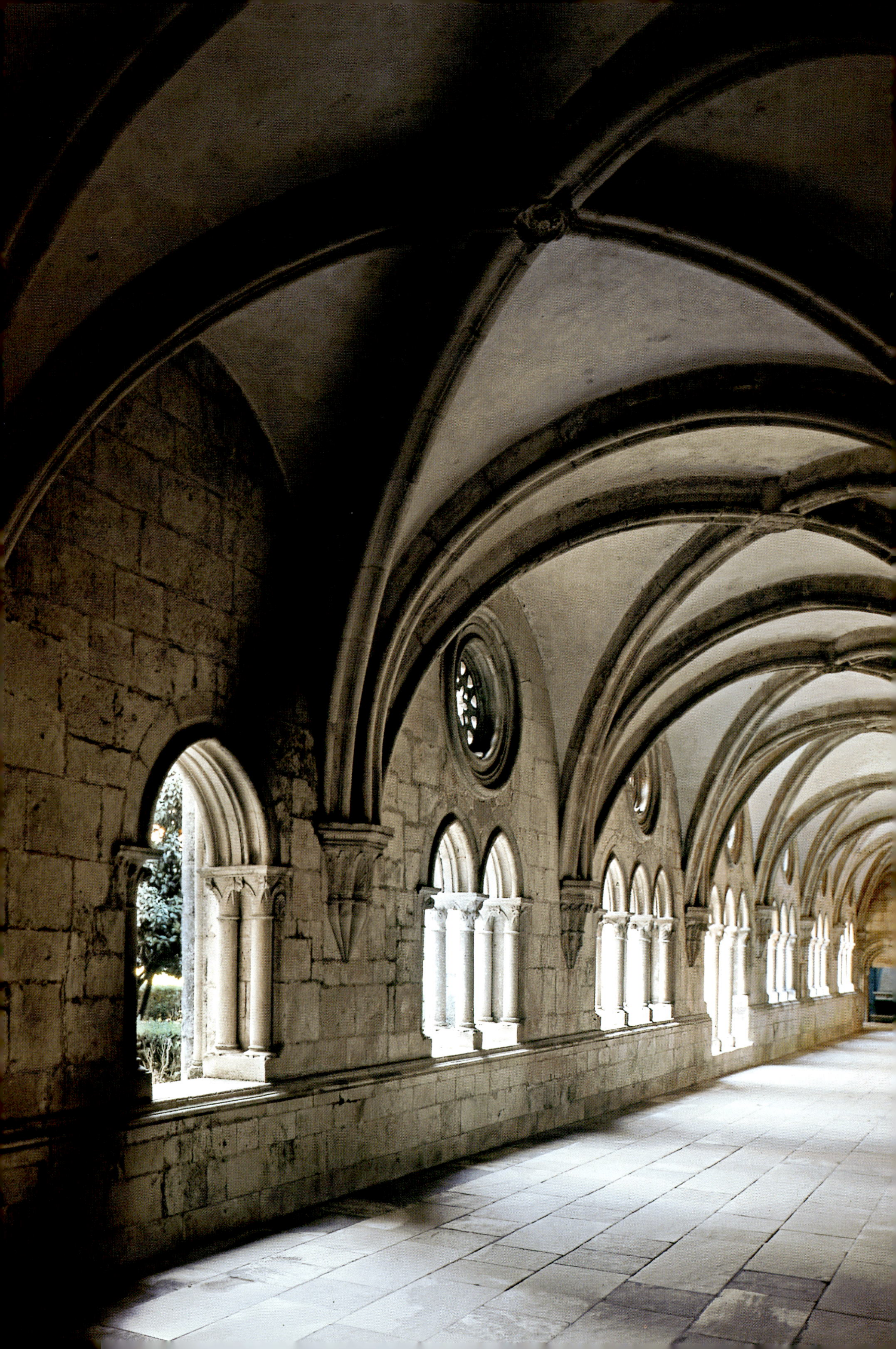

Gallery in the
Cloister of Silence

THE CLOISTER OF SILENCE

The main cloister of the monastic complex is so called because of the rule of silence the monks were obliged to keep, a rule that could only be broken in the parlour. It is the only medieval cloister at Alcobaça, and one of its most interesting buildings. Also known as the Cloister of King Dinis, as it was built during his reign (albeit with money bequeathed by King Afonso III in his will of 1271), it is one of the largest and most beautiful of the medieval Cistercian cloisters. According to an inscription on the wall facing the chapter house, work began in 1308 and was completed in September 1311. Its architects were Domingo Domingues and Mestre Diogo, and its structure is slightly irregular – largely due to the uneven site – but characteristically Cistercian. It is also the largest Gothic cloister in Portugal.

According to Cistercian practice, the cloister was referred to in the plural since its four wings were

Inscription next to the chapter house, alluding to the completion of the Cloister of Silence

The Refectory Cloister

The Lay Brothers' Cloister

The Refectory Cloister and the lavabo

Interior of the lavabo, from the Refectory Cloister

Basin in the lavabo

56   The Monastery of Alcobaça

each given a name that reflected its function. The south wing, next to the church, was the Reading Cloister, where, before the compline service, the monks listened to the abbot reading the *Collations* written by the founder and first abbot of St Victor's Abbey in Marseille. The Chapter Cloister, which was the wing of the chapter house, was to the east, while the Refectory Cloister served that building, on the north side. Finally, the west wing was traditionally identified as the Lay Brothers' Cloister. The significant transformation it underwent in modern times is described further on.

The irregularity of the construction is evident in the unequal number of bays: eight in the north wing and 10 in the south. The imposing polygonal structure housing the lavabo (the communal washing area) was built in the north wing, with six sides supported by buttresses and divided into two floors, which, according to Gusmão has 'the splendour of a large Gothic apse'.

The whole cloister is vaulted, with semicircular transverse arches and ogives formed by depressed arches, rounded ribs and bosses, some of which depict the Royal Coat of Arms. As a result of the slight asymmetry of the construction, the vaults are quite irregular in the north wing and even more so in the west wing. The height of the galleries is unequal for the same reason, with the lowest next to the wall of the church and the highest in the northwest corner, where the small round-arched door – with two colonnettes, side capitals and a tympanum with dentil mouldings – led to the original kitchen. Two more large semicircular arched doorways, which are closer in style to the Romanesque tradition that marked the beginning of the construction, give access to the medieval sacristy, which is next to the Chapter Cloister and to the Lay Brothers' Cloister in the west gallery, which has only recently been identified.

The various entrances onto the central courtyard from the cloister are also irregular. Arches stand on

Doorway leading to the original sacristy

Doorway leading to the medieval kitchen

58   The Monastery of Alcobaça

paired colonnettes crowned by capitals with plant, animal and anthropomorphic motifs, with some consisting of double openings with slightly pointed arches (Reading Cloister), some combining double and triple openings with the same type of arch (west gallery and the Chapter Cloister), and others having arches with a trefoil profile characteristic of the fourteenth century. In all cases, there is an oculus with elaborate moulding above (in many instances the result of recent restoration), and the whole is supported by substantial buttresses on the central courtyard side.

Thus, it is known for certain that the original chapter house was renovated when the Cloister of Silence was built. The large portal, with its four arcades and semicircular Romanesque arches, was retained, although with a more modest decoration consisting of simple plant motifs. The portal and the doors – all of them very similar – lining the cloister's entire outer wall and leading to the monks' choir, the sacristy, the parlour, the calefactory, the refectory, the kitchen and the lay brothers' wing are of clear Romanesque inspiration. The same is true of the corbels, placed on either side of the sacristy door leading to the chapter house to support the transverse arches and carry the ribs of the vaulted ceiling. This wall still bears some scars from the time parts of it were bricked up, and their presence could well lend credence to Cocheril's theory that this is, in fact, a 'reconstruction' of the cloister built in the reign of King Dinis.

This theory is based on the assumption that work on the earlier project would have begun with the south wing, next to the church. The south wing would have been vaulted and buttressed in order to support the church wall, since there were no buttresses on the church side. Construction would have continued around the courtyard, thus providing access to the various monastic buildings. It is likely that

Detail of niche, corbel and ribs in the Reading Cloister, with evidence of the scars on the outer wall of the church

The Cloister of Silence 59

only the roof above the Reading Cloister and above the Chapter Cloister adjacent to the chapter house would have been finished, since these parts of the building were most important to monastic life.

The cloister that was started late in the thirteenth century would have been completed during the reign of King Dinis. The need for extra structural support would have become apparent as work progressed towards the façade, in other words during the latter half of the thirteenth century, when the already existing constructions had been renovated and remodelled. Among the characteristics of the renovation are the long triple conical corbels on the wall on the courtyard side, which support the arches springing from the older corbels on the outer wall.

Between 1505 and 1519, and by order of Abbot Jorge de Melo before he became Bishop of Guarda, an upper gallery was built onto the cloister. It was the work of João de Castilho, in collaboration with Nicolau

Doorway leading to the temple, in the corner between the Reading Cloister and the Chapter Cloister

Triple conical corbel in the Cloister of Silence

Triple conical corbel, with more elaborate decoration, in the Cloister of Silence

The Cloister of Silence   61

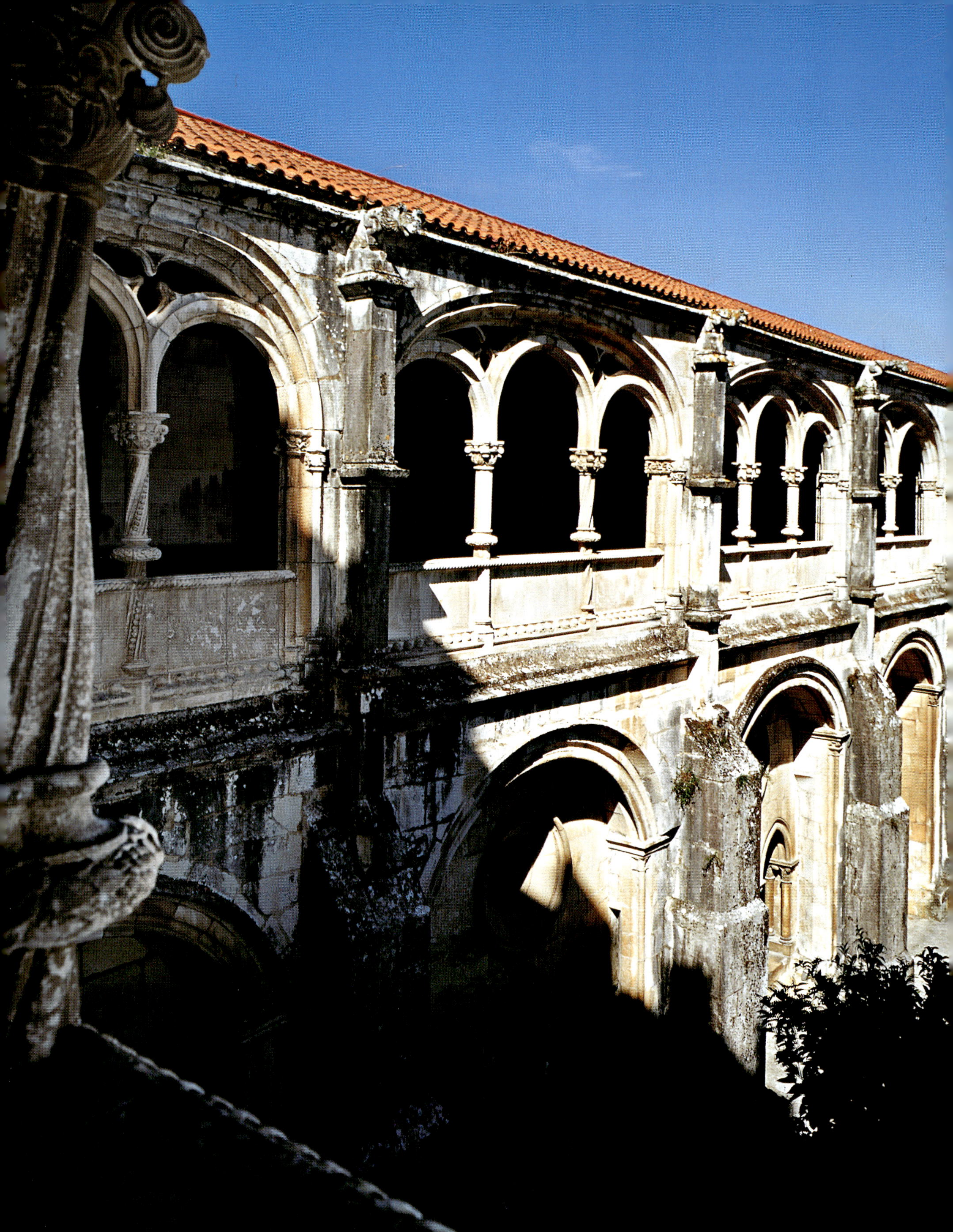

The upper gallery of the Cloister of Silence

Terrace of the lavabo, with a sundial from the modern period

Pires, and led to the extension of the buttresses up to roof level, where they were finished off by gargoyles. This gallery was reached from the Reading Cloister via a staircase situated close to its southeast corner. The small doorway leading to it can still be seen.

Made up of double and triple arches inserted into depressed apertures on characteristically Manueline colonnettes and capitals, the openings to the gallery added a note of elegance to the whole structure and allowed the development of new constructions on the upper floor, as well as access to the rooftop of the lavabo.

The Cloister of Silence 63

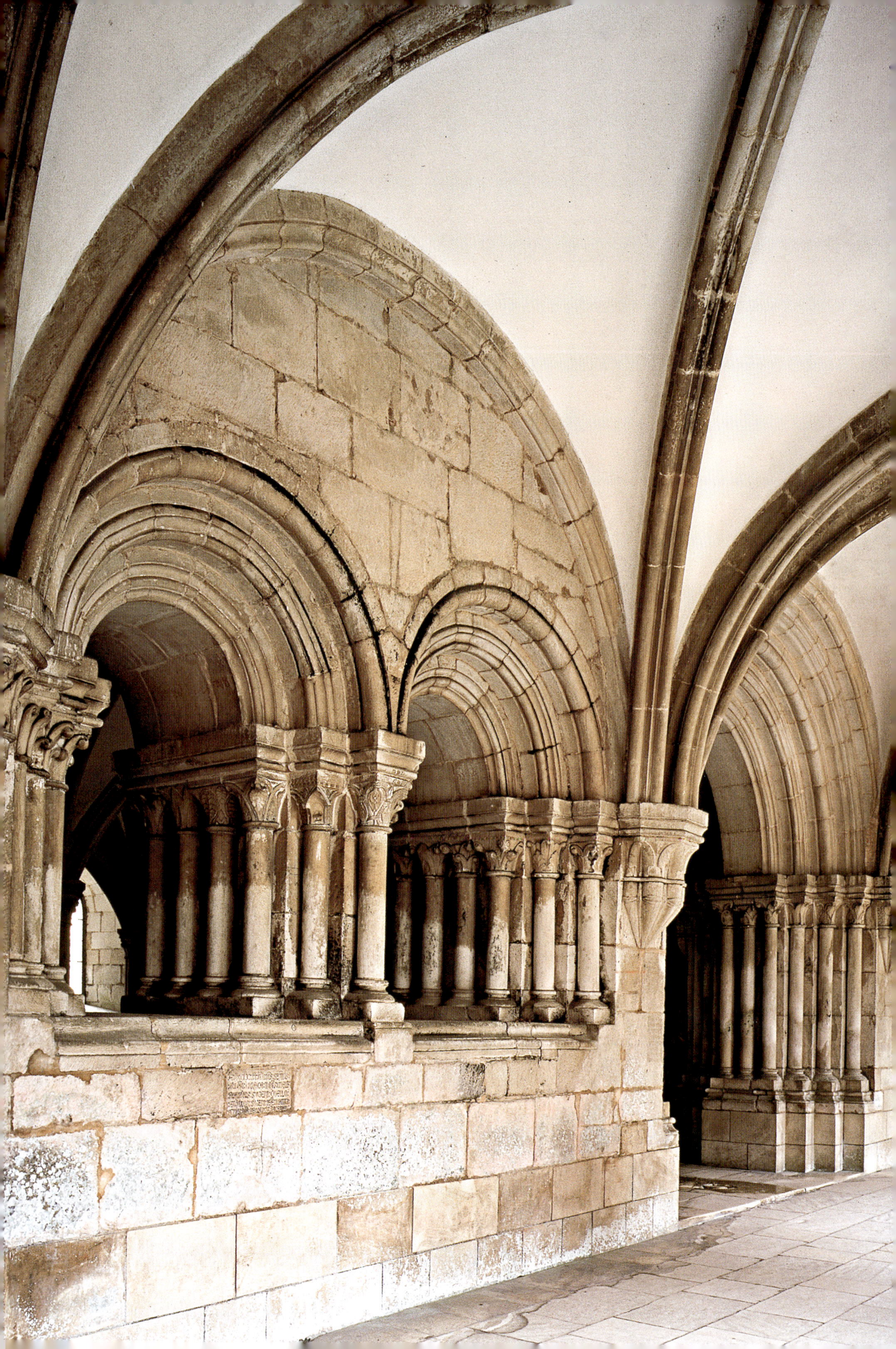

Exterior of the chapter house

THE CHAPTER HOUSE

The chapter house is one of the most important buildings of any monastery, being the place where the chapter of the congregation assembles. At Alcobaça it assumes particular importance due to the status of the monastery among the Portuguese Cistercians and the consequent size of its congregation.

It was here that all the significant matters relating to community life were dealt with, including those concerning the administration of the vast and lucrative, but economically and politically complex, area of land controlled by Alcobaça. It was the place where the abbot was elected and also where the distribution of labour was defined. The chapter house also provided the setting for monks to be heard on important questions and for sins to be confessed – in front of the assembled community – relating to failures in the strict observance of the Rule of St Benedict. It was also the place where government of the Order over its monastic houses was reasserted after the Restoration, re-establishing the Portuguese Cistercian Autonomous Congregation that had been created by King Sebastião in 1567. (This had come about via a Papal Bull of Pius V but until 1642 had been subject to the whims of royal power.)

Funeral inscription and depiction of a nobleman with the Sousa coat of arms on the outer face of the chapter-house wall

Artistically, the chapter house is a discernibly Gothic construction, adopting a style characteristic of royal commission from the time of King Dinis. It has parallels in other buildings in the Lisbon region, such as in the cloister of the capital's cathedral. In spite of this, a degree of archaism – or concession to the Romanesque tradition – is still evident. At its entrance, for example, a profusion of colonnettes and capitals of decidedly Gothic proportions and decoration are found side by side with the semicircular arches previously mentioned.

The virtually rectangular interior reveals the period of its construction in a less ambiguous manner, undoubtedly coinciding with the completion of the cloister in the first quarter of the fourteenth century. This is evident from the design of the roof, which has ogival vaults standing on a mesh of arches with a rounded profile. These spring from four bundles of eight colonnettes each and end in corbels with conical lower parts, also grouped in bundles, in the exterior walls of the chapter house. The corbels are identical in every way to those of the final phase of construction of the cloister.

A stone bench for the monks to sit on ran around the exterior walls, and three windows on the east side provided light.

Interior and entranceway of the chapter house

The chapter house

Tomb of the Abbot of Alcobaça, at the entrance to the chapter house

The Chapter House 67

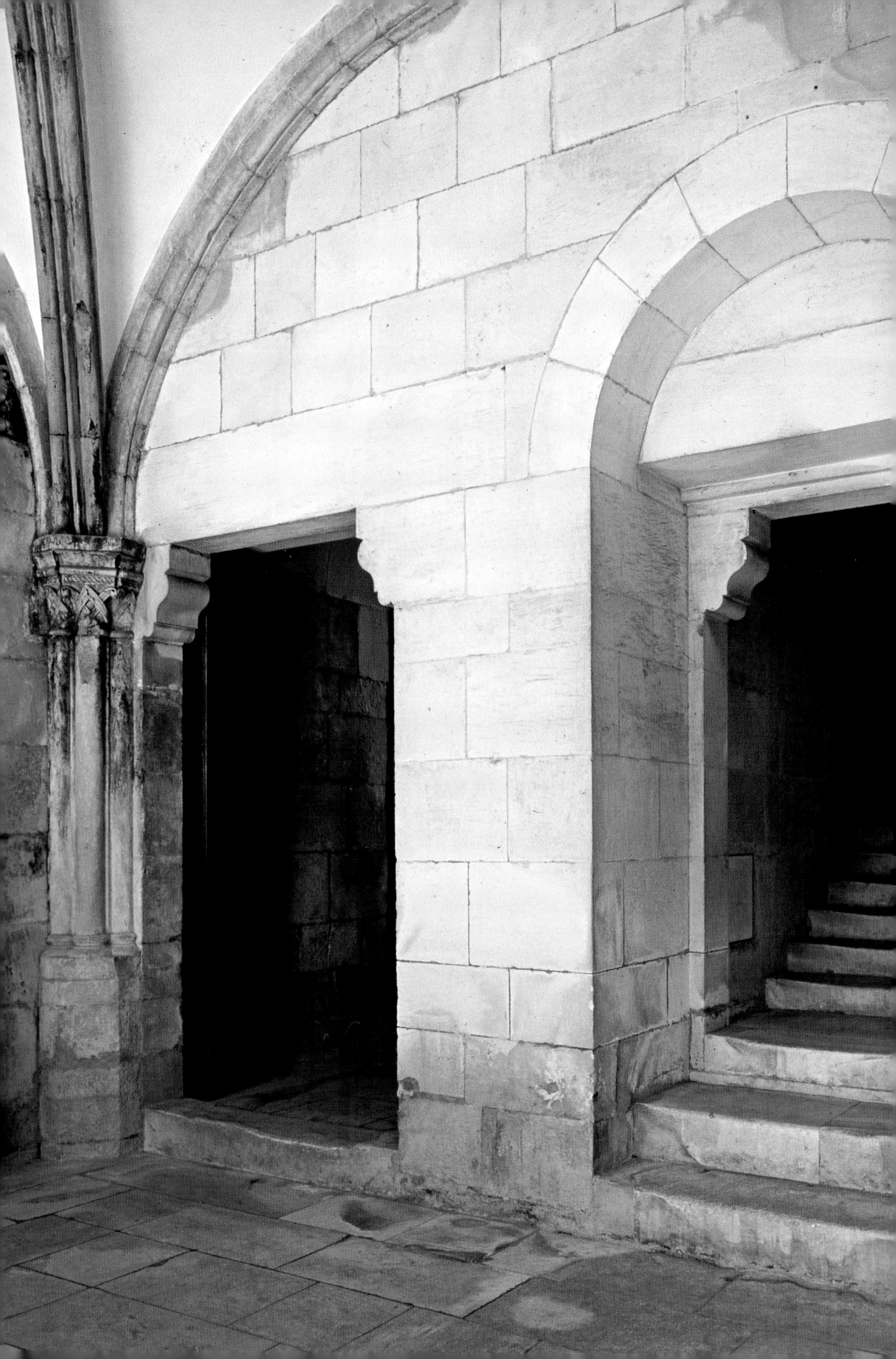

Doorways leading to the dormitory staircase (right) and to the Monks' Hall, in the corner of the Chapter Cloister and Refectory Cloister

THE PARLOUR

On the north side of the chapter house, and sharing with it a partition wall, is the parlour, also known as the Prior's Parlour as it was where the prior remained behind to hear the monks after the daily meeting of the chapter. It was one of the few places in the monastery where it was permitted, albeit briefly, to break the rule of silence.

Architecturally, it is a long narrow room, the same depth as the chapter house at just over 17 metres. A door at one end led outside to the infirmary, which, for health reasons, was built apart from the rest of the buildings.

Its most unusual detail is its roof, which boasts a three-bay ogival crossed-rib vault, although the middle bay has been rebuilt as a groin vault, undoubtedly to lower the rear section to make room for the turn in the staircase. The stairs, located on the north side of this room, give access to the dormitory on the upper floor.

THE MONKS' HALL

Forming the easternmost point of this trident of rooms is the Monks' Hall, a common structure in many monasteries of the Order, the function of which, however, is not entirely clear. It is possible, as Cocheril suggests, that it was designed in the medieval period to house novices, a function we know that it fulfilled in the late fifteenth century and one which was only abandoned when the dormitories and the Novices' Cloister were built.

Structurally, this room suffers from the uneven nature of the site of the monastic complex. Its floor is made up of five platforms that descend from the entrance towards the outside wall, which is pierced by two large windows to let in light. Openings in the wall separating the room from the calefactory (now the kitchen) provided more light. On the south wall there is a small room, a structure also common to other monastic complexes, which may have served as a parlour for the novices.

This vast space is more than 32 metres long and similar in width to the chapter house and parlour, with which it is aligned. From an architectural point of view, it is without doubt the most characteristically utilitarian space of this whole wing of the cloister. It is covered by a vaulted roof supported on ribs with a square profile, with sharp edges, standing on 10 thick columns – two for each level of the ground space. The columns are adorned with a very simple plant decoration on the capitals, and finish, at the external walls, with corbels, most of which have an equally simple prismatic base.

Although the whole construction is robust in appearance, the regular pattern of the columns and ribs, and the way in which they increase in height as the floor level declines, lend it a certain elegance. This keeps the level of the roof constant and creates, with the false perspective introduced by the growing distance between floor and vault, the sense of a room of greater magnitude and elegance.

Following page
Interior of the Monks' Hall

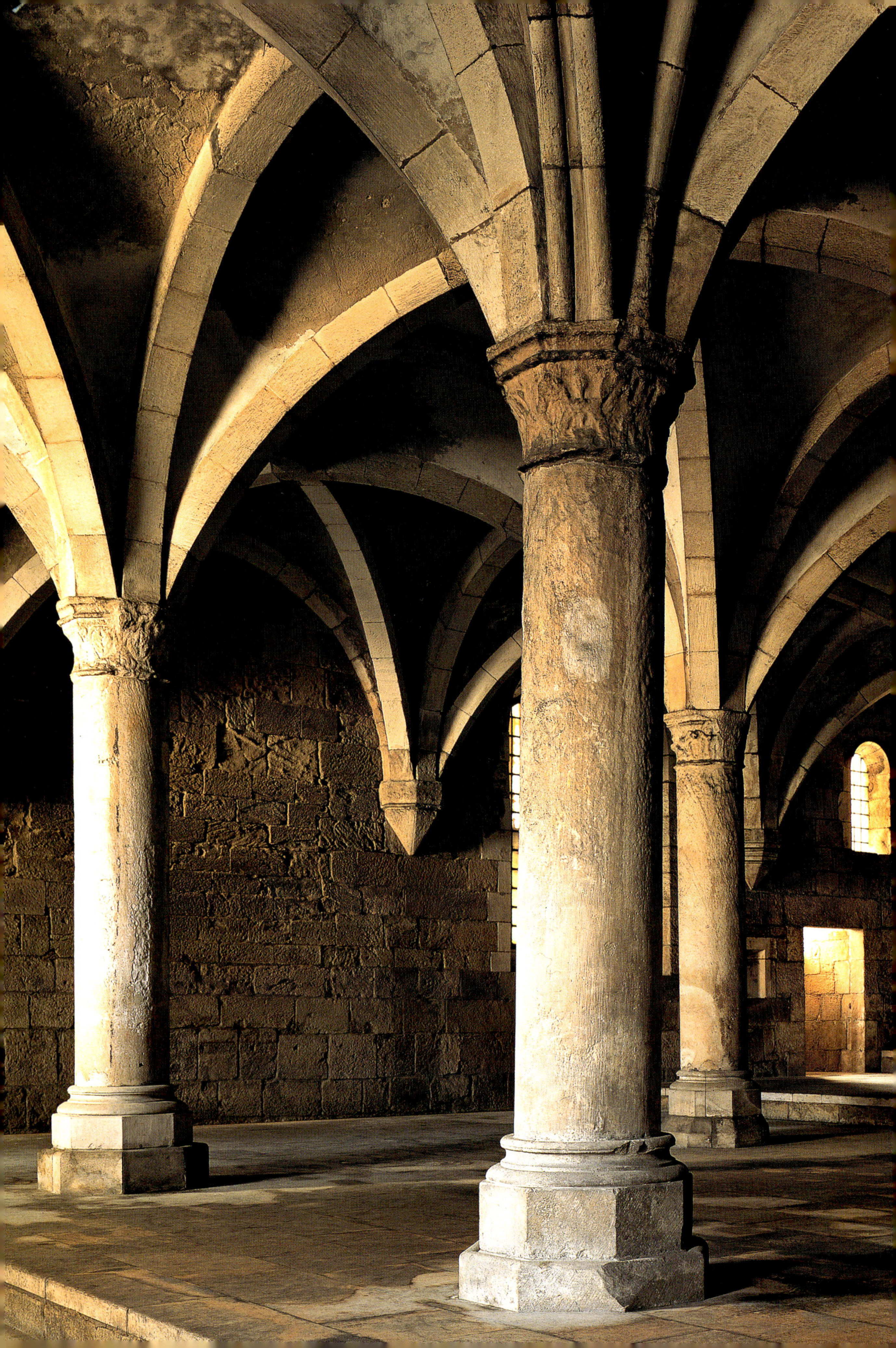

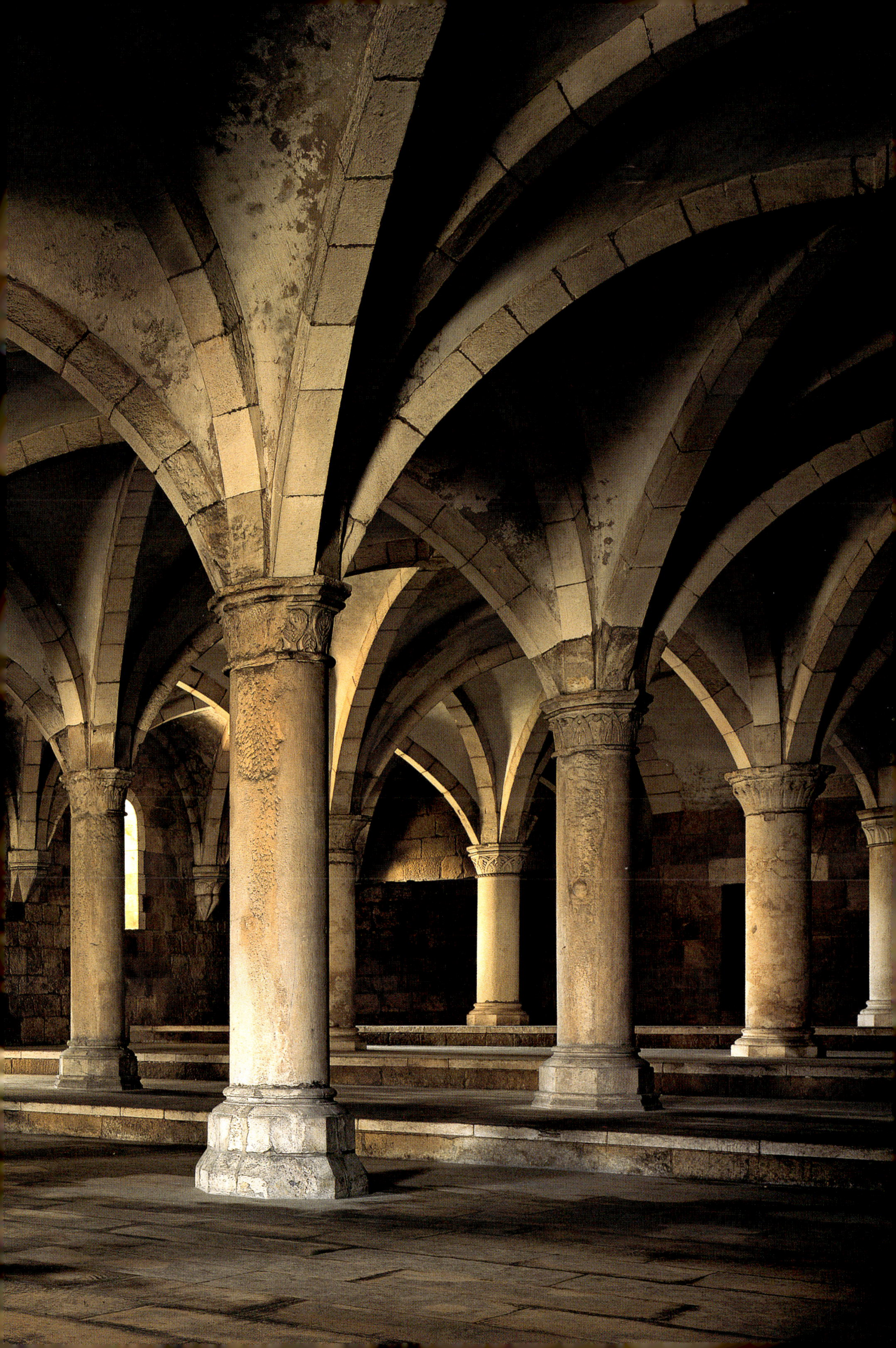

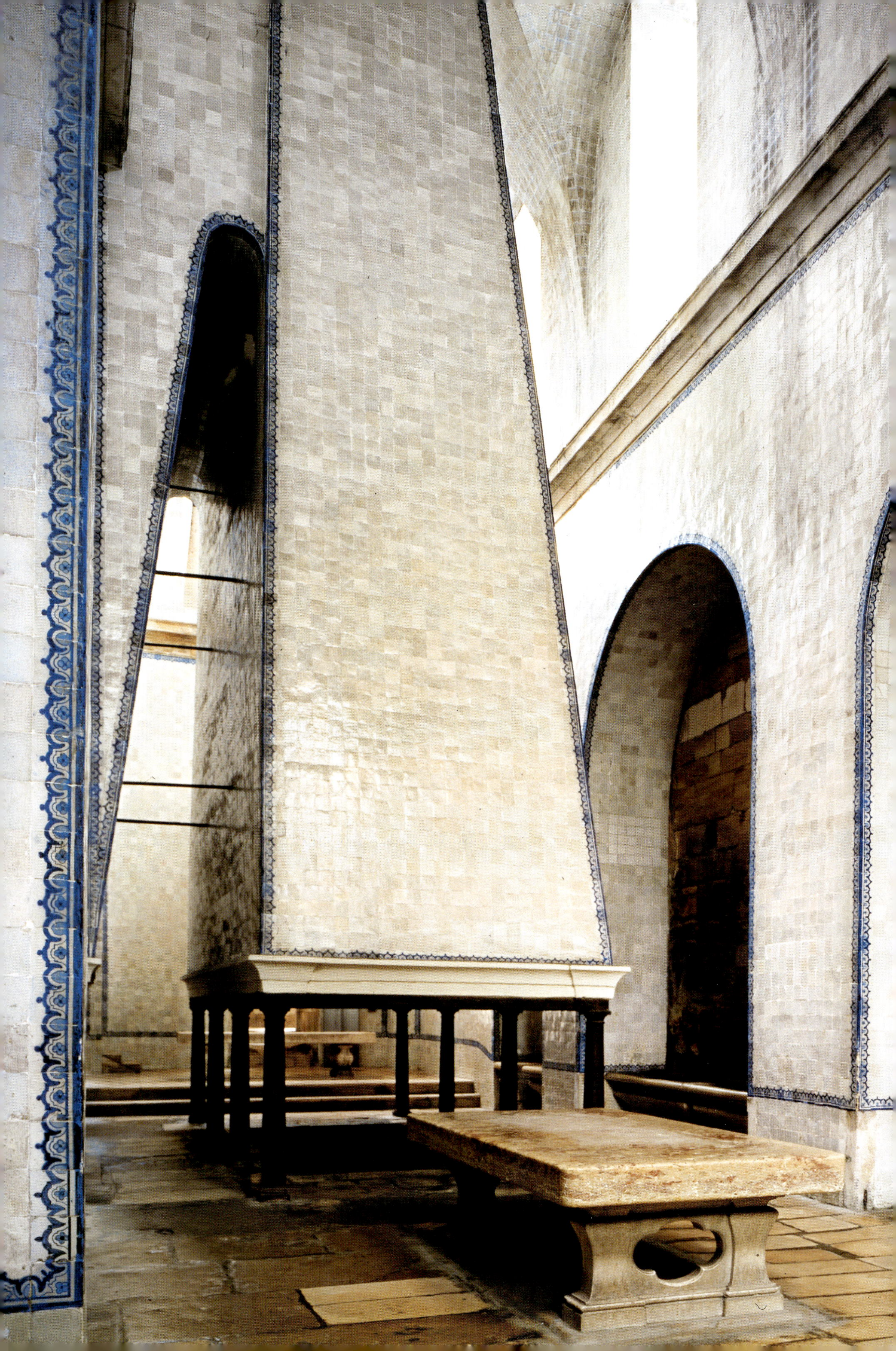

Interior of the modern kitchen, showing the tile-lined chimney

THE KITCHEN

The original medieval kitchen was situated on the west side of the refectory but was most probably destroyed in the third quarter of the seventeenth century, when King Afonso VI ordered a small cloister to be built there. All that remains is the medieval door, which is Romanesque in appearance and opens onto the northwest corner of the cloister.

Recent archaeological excavations have, however, unearthed some of the structures of this original kitchen, notably a system of channels that was later used to supply water to the kitchen. They have also uncovered a series of curious stone supports on various levels, which are carved with cyma mouldings and function as corbels to support the kitchen structure.

The present kitchen, located on the opposite side of the refectory, between the medieval refectory and

Doorway leading to the former calefactory, later to become the kitchen

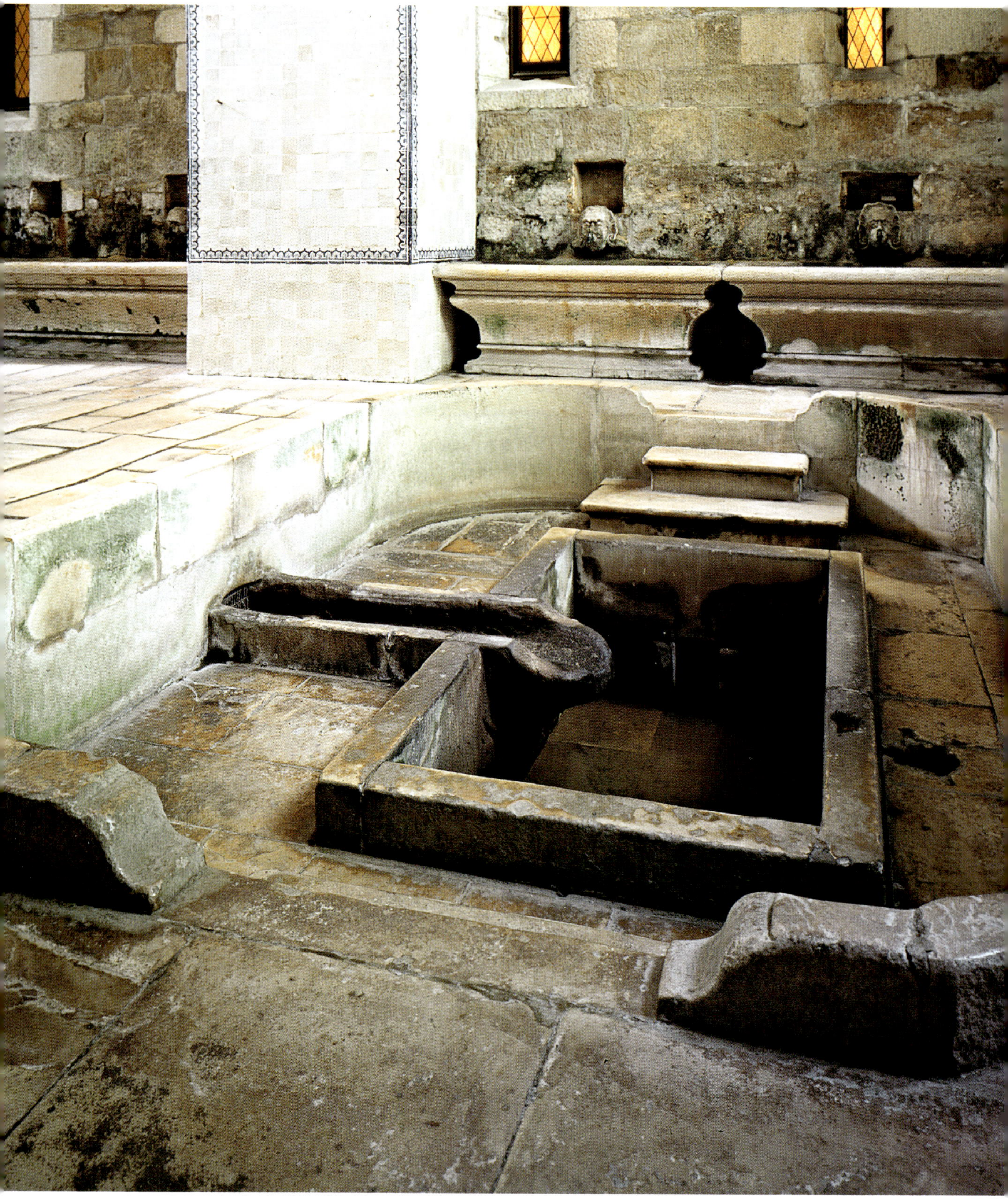

Tank in the kitchen, fed by a branch of the *levada*

Detail of the kitchen ceiling lined in white tiles

the Monks' Hall, is a modern construction. It was erected on the former site of the monastery's calefactory, which became obsolete with the building of monks' cells and new dormitory blocks with more modern and effective heating arrangements. It can be reached through the medieval calefactory doorway, under two round archivolts that are elegantly supported on the outer side by a pair of colonnettes with plant-decorated capitals.

The simplicity of the entranceway is at odds with the extraordinary sight inside: a room nearly 30 metres long and over 18 metres high. The large chimney in the centre is lined with *azulejos* dating back to 1752, resembling those lining the interior walls. The structure is supported by eight neo-classical columns and their respective architraves. Modelled in cast iron, they are undoubtedly among the first structures in Portugal to be made from this material.

The kitchen also houses the large tank in which water was stored for washing and cooking (an abundant supply of water being particularly important to the Cistercians), as well as the imposing stone tables and side tanks. The original medieval walls and their openings can still be seen behind the eighteenth-century structure of the present kitchen.

The great stone table and chimney in the kitchen

The Kitchen 75

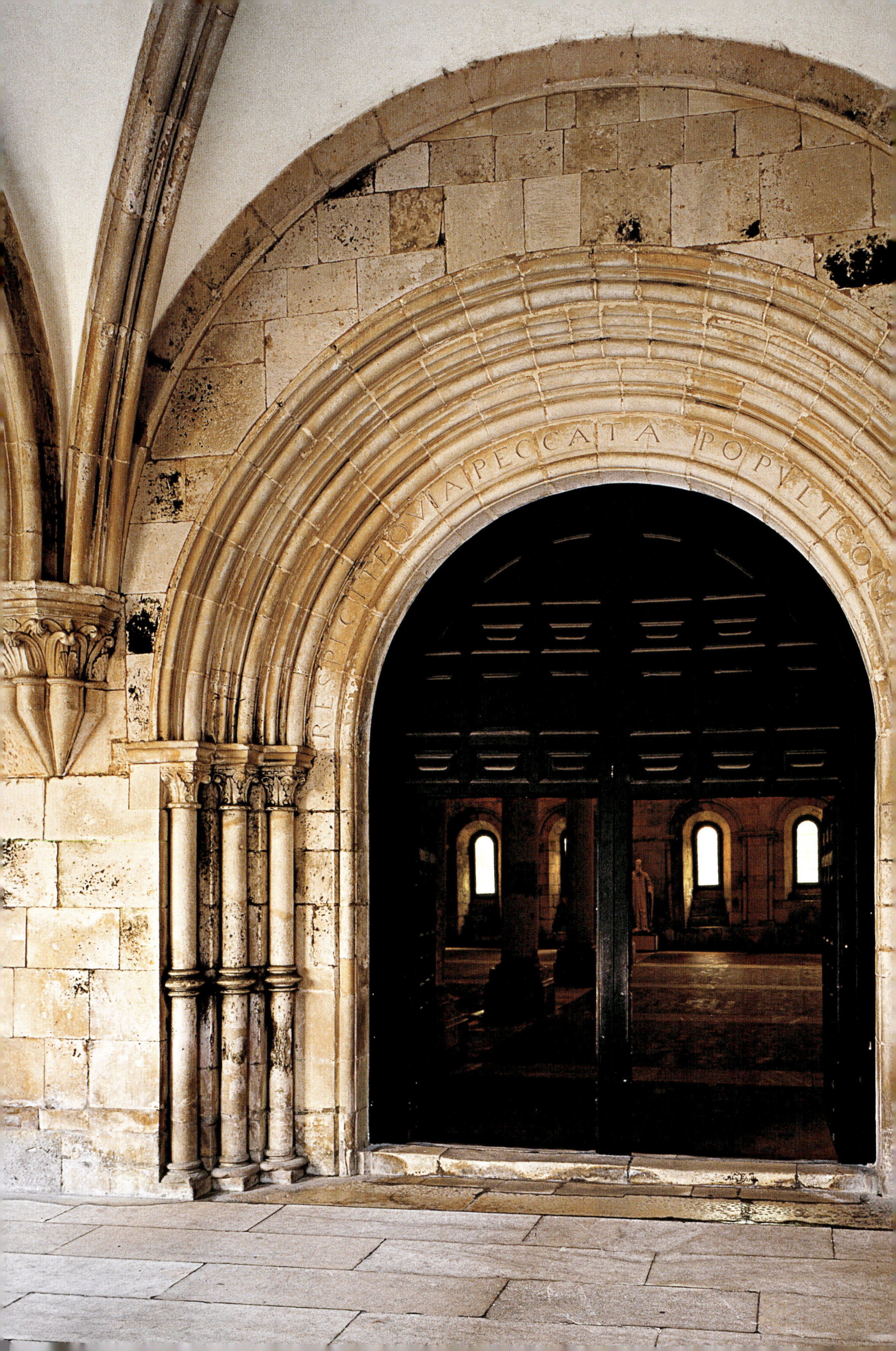
RESPICITE QVIA PECCATA POPVLI CO

Doorway leading
to the refectory

THE REFECTORY

Located to the side of the present kitchen, the medieval refectory is one of the most interesting of the monastery's buildings in terms of dimensions, architectural and decorative treatment, and structural complexity. Its entrance is via a large semicircular arch – under three archivolts on colonnettes with plant-patterned capitals – bearing the inscription in Vulgar Latin:

Respicite Qvia Peccata Popvli Comeditis (Be aware that you eat the sins of the people).

It is a building of particularly harmonious proportions. The same length as the new kitchen, at just over 21 metres wide, its size ratio is approximately 3:2. It is also similar in height to the new kitchen, although it is divided into two levels.

It has three aisles of five bays, divided by two rows of four extremely elegant columns ending in

The refectory, viewed from the entrance

78   The Monastery of Alcobaça

The refectory, viewed from the front wall

Capital on a column in the refectory, decorated with a plant motif and an octagonal abacus

Triple conical corbel on the side wall of the refectory

octagonal capitals. The columns stand on square bases and are both narrower and taller than those in the Monks' Hall. Their capitals are decorated with plant designs of a very high calibre, including well-sculpted and voluminous crockets and leaves.

Despite the general quality of the construction, there appears to have been some hesitation when work began. This is evident in the irregular arrangement of the lower part, especially in the section alongside the wall that overlooks the cloister. Cocheril even ventures the theory that the present crossed-rib vault, composed of ogives with quadrangular ribs similar to those in the Monks' Hall, may have been preceded by an earlier wooden one, which would explain why the vestiges of a cornice can still be seen on the walls.

The room, which would have contained tables for meal sittings, is lit mainly by the broad windows in the façade at the north end. The six windows on the lower level and the two on the upper level above the side aisles are surmounted by a large round oculus that opens onto the central nave. The eight windows in the east wall and four in the west, of varying dimensions and positions, brought additional light to the refectory, but some of these are now walled up.

The most interesting and original feature of the refectory is the famous reader's pulpit, located almost in the northwest corner of the west wall, where a monk would read aloud from sacred texts during meals. Accessing the pulpit via a flight of stairs, one is met at the top by five arches, complete with elaborately executed colonnettes and capitals. To the side, and closer to the corner, are two further passages: one undoubtedly led to the adjoining medieval kitchen, and the other is thought to have led outside to the kitchen yard.

Lateral wall of the refectory, showing the elaborate reader's pulpit

The Refectory

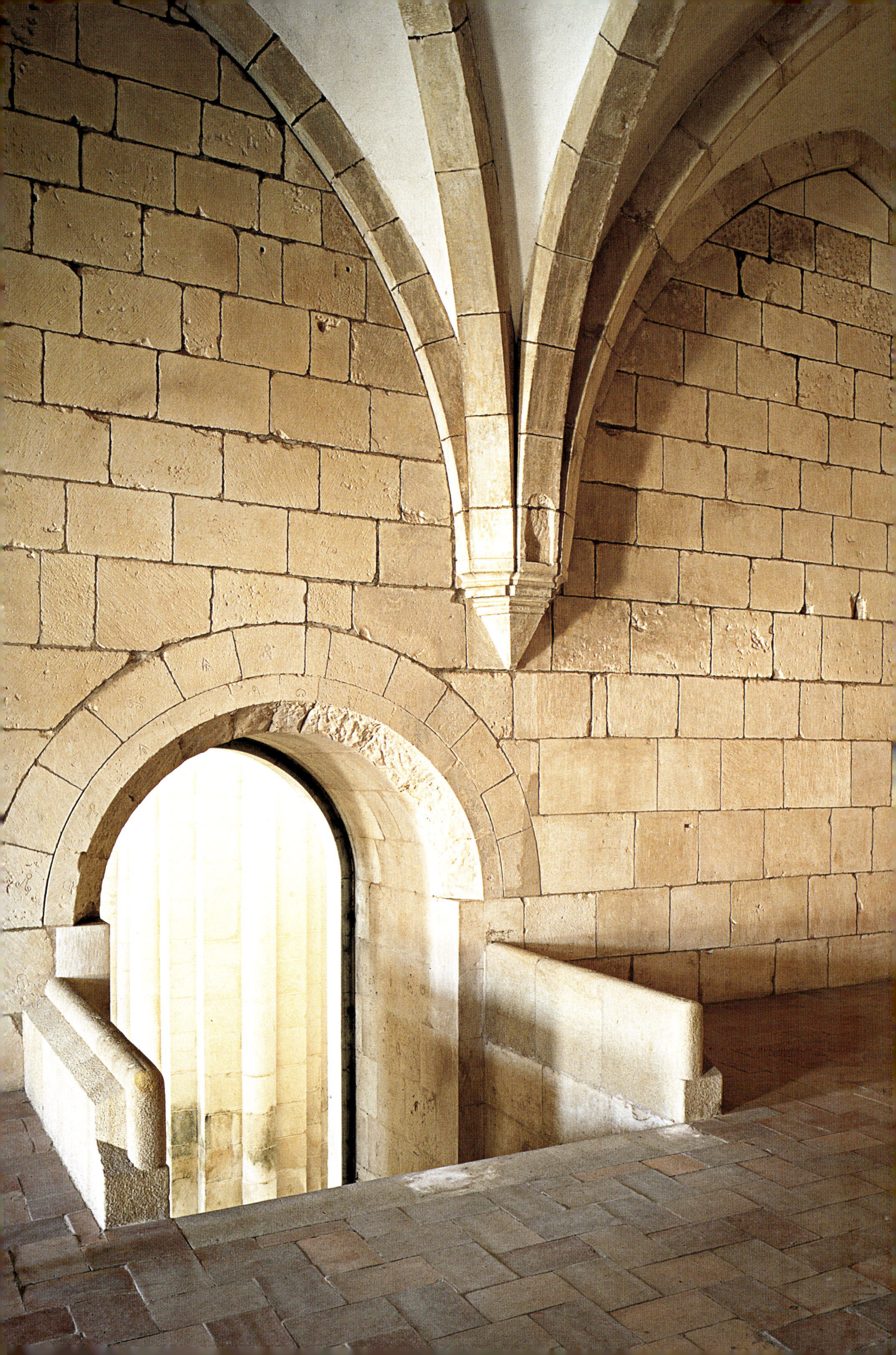

South wall of the dormitory, showing the entrance to the Matins Staircase (*Escada das Matinas*)

THE MONKS' DORMITORY

Completing the set of medieval rooms is the Monks' Dormitory, reached via a staircase between the parlour and the Monks' Hall, and with direct access to the transept of the church, as was usual in most Cistercian monasteries.

It is a long room occupying the entire first floor of the Chapter Cloister, almost 67 metres in length. It is divided into three aisles of 11 bays by thick sturdy columns similar to those in the Monks' Hall. These columns are topped by octagonal capitals decorated with plant motifs, upon which ribs of quadrangular cross-section similar to those in the Monks' Hall and the refectory support an ogival crossed-rib vault. In addition to the pyramid-base corbels supporting the ribs, the west wall boasts a series of narrow openings to provide light. Along with the large windows on the opposite wall, which are considerably thick, it was

The Monks' Dormitory

Capital of dormitory column decorated with plant motifs

Capital of dormitory column decorated with stylised plant motifs

Capital of dormitory column decorated with a continuous ribbon motif

82 The Monastery of Alcobaça

Capital of dormitory column decorated with a plaiting motif

Capital of dormitory column decorated with large stylised leaf motifs

Capital of dormitory column decorated with voluminous crocket leaf motifs

The Monks' Dormitory

Partial view of the Monks' Dormitory, to the west

Eastern wall of the dormitory, with French windows leading to the Cardinal's Cloister

84   The Monastery of Alcobaça

possible to keep the interior reasonably warm.

While this arrangement has been retained on the west wall (along with the small niches beside each bed), on the east wall the façade was completely altered and new broad windows installed as a result of the sixteenth-century construction of the new Novices' Cloister

On the north wall there were several windows that were bricked up due to the reinforcement of the buttresses or piers on the outside. Next to the church wall, in an area where the dormitory is extended into a further aisle, there is a window at the side of the original door (also walled up) that gave the monks direct access to the north transept via the Matins Staircase.

A puzzling aspect of the medieval buildings at Alcobaça, particularly noticeable here in the dormitory, is the apparent contradiction between the rather archaic style of its structure, with its distinctly Romanesque features, and what appears to be a later style adopted for the chapter house situated beneath it. Equally curious is the unevenness of the levels that provide access to the church, and of the stairway to the cloister: the stairway curves sideways, which meant that modifications had to be made to the parlour roof. By comparison, the dormitory floor, which is positioned a good deal higher up, is level, as is also the case at Fontenay.

With no definitive data to explain these anomalies, one explanation may be that the present dormitory is of a later date than it appears. It may be the case that it was built after the construction of the chapter house and close in time to the other medieval sections such as the Monks' Hall and the refectory (thought to be between the late thirteenth and early fourteenth centuries). The design variations in the chapter house might be seen to be the result of 'positive discrimination', in other words, that more elaborate architecture was used to reflect a nobler function.

North side of the Monks' Dormitory

Our Lady of the Conception with Symbols relating to the Immaculate Conception, by Baltazar Gomes Figueira, c. 1650

In the modern period, and particularly during the eighteenth century, the monastery underwent various alterations and additions to the entire west façade, completing the transformation that began in the sixteenth century. The new library, the Hall of the Kings, the new pantheon, and an immense collection of polychrome terracotta statuary depicting angels, Apostles and other sacred figures – including a remarkable Virgin and a representation of St Bernard himself – date from this period.

The pieces in polychrome lacquered wood are also noteworthy, especially those of the Infantas Teresa and Sancha, St Umbelina (sister of St Bernard), and *Our Lady of the Rosary*, a piece of exceptional Baroque design which probably dates from 1753 to 1762 and is now in the chancel. Other pieces include depictions of St Sebastian, also in polychrome wood, and a remarkable set of terracotta pieces, notably a representation of St John.

There is also a set of exquisite paintings, including several attributed to Josefa de Óbidos and her father, Baltazar Gomes Figueira, such as *Our Lady of the Conception with Symbols relating to the Immaculate Conception*, which the monastery commissioned him to paint around 1650. All these pieces date from the more recent decoration of the complex but there are many remarkable works that predate them.

Along with *Our Lady of the Rosary*, two other representations of the Virgin are particularly noteworthy. Firstly, the *Virgin of the Cloister*, so called because it stands on an elaborate altar cut into the wall of the church in the Reading Cloister. The altar is decorated with floral medallions in bas-relief framed by two Solomonic or twisted columns; it imitates the design of an eighteenth-century carved wooden altar, although here it is made of stone. The image itself is also made of polychrome stone and stands at over a metre and a half in height. It is a rare and beautiful piece of sixteenth-century statuary attributed to

Altar, showing the *Virgin of the Cloister* in the Reading Cloister

Nicholas de Chanterenne, the great French Renaissance sculptor who produced a considerable amount of work in Portugal during the first half of the sixteenth century.

The other image, also of stone and dating from the fifteenth century, is smaller and stands in the Hall of the Kings. It is known as *Our Lady of the Castle* or *Our Lady of the Rock*, indicating that it probably came from the town's first church, which was built within the town's castle.

Among the remaining statuary, all Baroque and predominantly from the second half of the seventeenth century, is a group that survived the dismantling of the large high altar. Like the group of the 'Death of St Bernard' or the statues of the great reliquary, these were made from terracotta by artist monks – the famous 'clay-figure makers of Alcobaça' – during the abbacy of Friar Sebastião de Sottomayor, between 1675 and 1678.

The remaining statues, over two and a half metres high, were made using the technique of successively superimposed 'layers' that the clay-figure makers employed. Identifiable by their inscriptions, today they stand in the chapter house. They are in a reasonable state of conservation and can be recognised as St Malachi, Archbishop of Armagh (Ireland) and friend of St Bernard; St Gregory the Great, sixth-century Pope; St Benedict, mentor of the Benedictine Order who drew up its Rule; St Thomas, archbishop of Canterbury; St Eugenius III, a Pope of Cistercian origin; and St Stephen Harding, third abbot of Citeaux.

Terracotta statues of St Benedict, St Gregory the Great and St Malachi

Terracotta statues of St Thomas, St Eugenius, St Bernard and St Stephen Harding

88   The Monastery of Alcobaça

Terracotta statue of an angel at the entrance to the chapter house

Alongside these are other statues depicting angels in various attitudes.

Several more images in polychrome wood reside in the radiating chapels of the ambulatory. On the south side are representations of St Joachim, the Virgin's father; St Anna, the Virgin's mother; the Virgin Mary herself; Jesus as an adult; and Jesus' father, St Joseph. In one of the last two chapels on the north side, which was formerly dedicated to St Bartholomew (as an inscription on the wall shows) are the images of St Umbelina, the sister of St Bernard. The last chapel was always dedicated to St Stephen and holds an image of him. All of these images come from altars that are no longer in existence and were placed in their current locations in recent times.

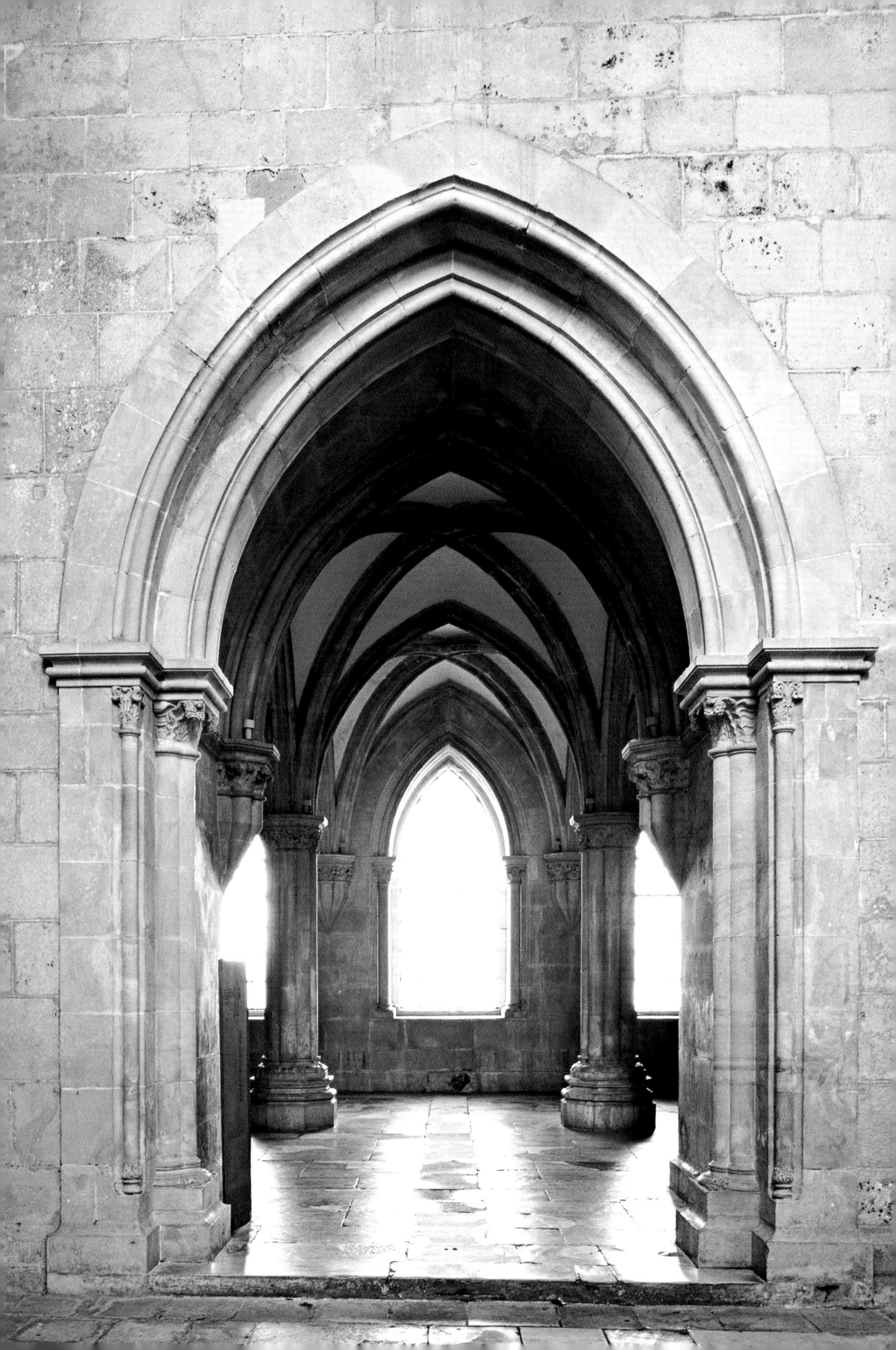

Entrance to the pantheon from the south transept

THE PANTHEON

Also known as the Hall of Tombs, this work was instigated by Abbot Friar Manuel de Mendonça and completed in 1782. It was designed to house the tombs that had been housed in the transept, which, along with the tombs of King Pedro and Inês de Castro, included the sarcophagi of Dona Urraca, Dona Beatriz and various princes and princesses, including the children of Afonso II, Dona Constança, daughter of Afonso III and probably Dom Dinis, son of Afonso IV.

These tombs, three of which are particularly remarkable, are clearly Romanesque in character, even though they date from well into the thirteenth century.

The first is a medium-sized, unidentified coffin that is decorated with plant motifs consistent with the Cistercian style of decoration, in which palm leaves and curled stems form designs similar to those

Small tomb decorated with stylised plant motifs

Tomb decorated with plant motifs in the form of palm leaves and curled stems

Small tomb of a child decorated with figures under arcades

Tomb, thought to be that of Queen Urraca

Tomb, thought to be that of Queen Beatriz

Partial view of the neo-Gothic hall of the pantheon

used in the margins of the illuminated manuscripts produced in the monastery's scriptorium.

Another sarcophagus, small in size and therefore probably belonging to one of the young princes, is decorated with a series of figures beneath arcades, characteristic of some Romanesque tombs.

The most important piece is the tomb that Manuel Real believes to be that of Dona Urraca, the wife of King Afonso II and mother of Sancho II and Afonso III. This is disputed, however, by José Custódio Vieira da Silva, who claims it is the tomb of Dona Beatriz, second wife of King Afonso III. It is an elaborate work, with a recumbent statue of the queen on the lid, with her hands crossed over her chest. At either end, two scenes are illustrated in bas-relief. At the head, the queen is depicted seated, with her hand to her face, flanked by what Carlos Alberto Ferreira de Almeida interprets as mourners. She appears to be sleeping or is more probably reflecting on her sins. At the other end is a depiction of the Christ Pantocrator, also in the Romanesque manner. On both sides, beneath six round arcades, are the figures of the Apostles, also in bas-relief. They are depicted in a rather clumsy and disproportionate way, as are the figures at either end; the legs appear too long and the whole is of an inferior quality to the sculpture of the three-dimensional recumbent figure on the lid.

The pantheon is the work of William Elsden, a cabinet-maker or joiner of English origin who apparently came to Portugal before 1763 at the behest of the Marquês de Pombal. He revealed himself to be a skilful military engineer, a role he executed whilst in Portugal. According to José Custódio Vieira da Silva, the work in Alcobaça was carried out after 1770, probably during the 1780s. Bearing in mind the function of the building, as well as the strong character of the medieval complex, Elsden displayed a near perfect ability to reproduce the style of the other buildings, creating with archaeological precision the forms and structures of the pointed architecture of the cloister and chapter house, even down to the Gothic inscriptions that can be found there.

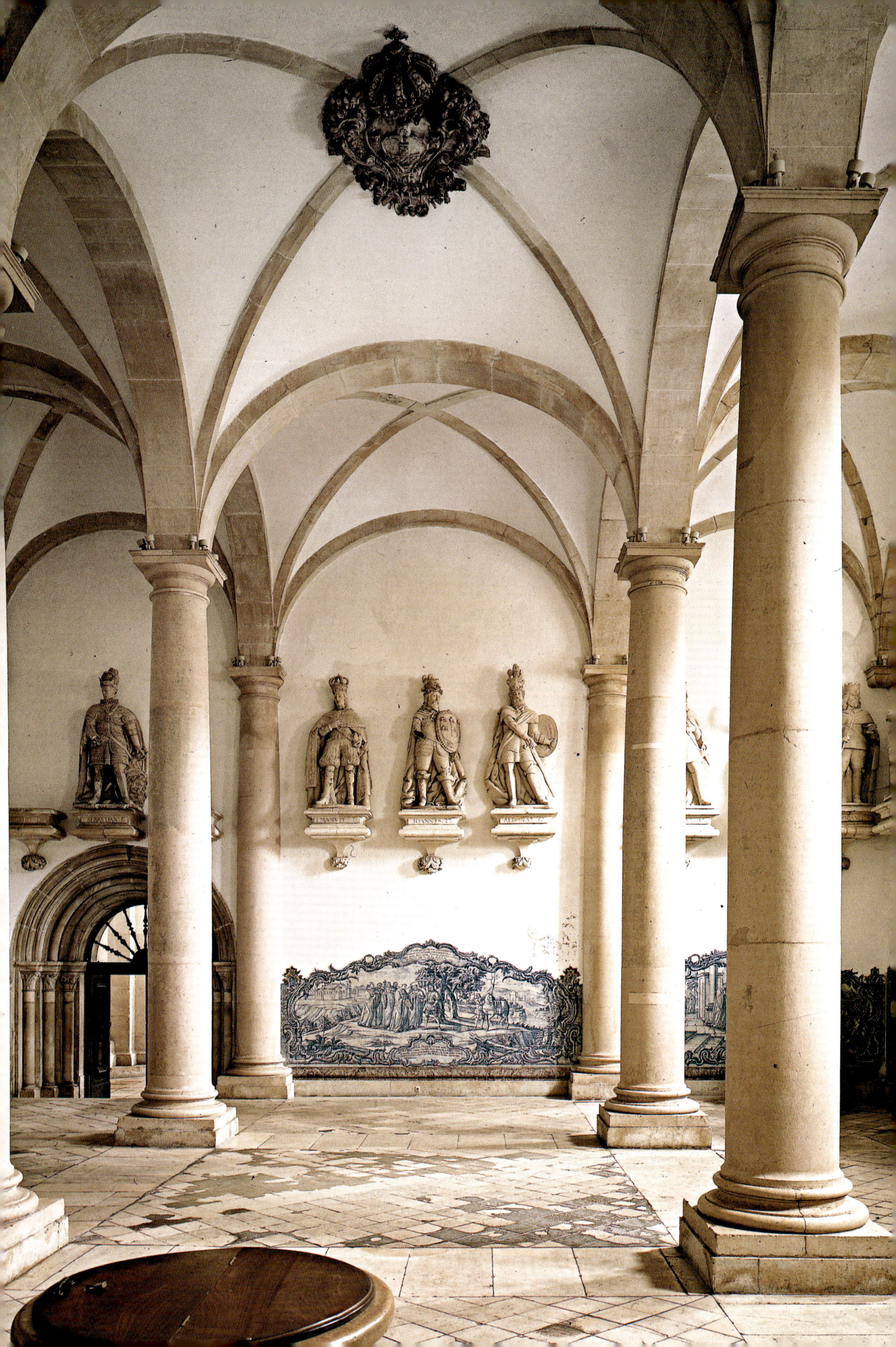

Interior of the
Hall of the Kings

THE HALL OF THE KINGS

Situated on the north side of the church façade, the Hall of the Kings (*Sala dos Reis*) is one of the most remarkable results of the eighteenth-century renovations, with its simple and unadorned classical architecture, precise proportions and occasional Renaissance allusions. Rafael Moreira suggests that it might originally have been an external church used to accommodate outsiders wishing to attend services. It was designed by Miguel de Arruda and built by Pêro Gomes in the second half of the sixteenth century. It is thought that it may have been modelled on the Church of Santa Maria at Estremoz, although this has been difficult to prove.

Doorway leading to
the Hall of the Kings,
from the Lay Brothers'
Cloister

This part of the monastery is most remarkable for its decoration and symbolism. There is a system of panels of *azulejos*, from the factory at Juncal and dating from after 1770, positioned around the lower part of the walls. The images on the panels relate passages from the legend of the founding of the monastery, interspersed by inscriptions taken from the *Chronica de Cister* (*Chronicle of Citeaux*) by Friar Bernardo de Brito.

There are 10 panels, starting in the northeast corner of the room:

Tiled panel depicting images of the legend of the founding of the monastery: 'Vow made by King Afonso Henriques'

Tiled panel depicting images of the legend of the founding of the monastery: 'St. Bernard praying with his monks'

96   The Monastery of Alcobaça

- *Vow made by the King, Dom Afonso Henriques, to found the Royal Monastery of Alcobaça if he achieved victory, by intercession of St Bernard, and the conquest of the town of Santarém, marching to this purpose in company of His brother the Infante Dom Pedro with only 250 armed men.*

- *St Bernard learning by revelation from Heaven of the vow that the King, Dom Afonso Henriques, has made to found Alcobaça and accepting it under the conditions in which it was made, implores God, along with his Monks, to bring success to the undertaking of the Portuguese.*

- *Five Monks come to Coimbra from Clairvaux, along with the Portuguese Nobleman, and they hand over the response of St Bernard to the King, Dom Afonso Henriques.*

- *He leaves, and the King, Dom Afonso Henriques, takes the town of Santarém, with 250 Portuguese men.*

Tiled panel depicting images of the legend of the founding of the monastery: 'King Afonso Henriques captures Santarém and St. Bernard announces the news at Clairvaux'

- *St Bernard gives news to his Monks at Clairvaux of the Letter from the King, Dom Afonso Henriques, informing him of the Conquest of Santarém, and he asks the monks to fulfil the vow, when already the Saint knew this fortune, and he sends the Monks to found this Illustrious and Royal Monastery of Alcobaça and gives them the measurements for this.*

- *They show to the King, Dom Afonso Henriques, and to the five Monks the outlines that St Bernard has given them of the site for the new Monastery on the field that is today called Chaqueda, and on it they mark the lines for its foundation.*

Tiled panel depicting images of the legend of the founding of the monastery: 'St. Bernard receives the letter from King Afonso Henriques'

Tiled panel depicting images of the legend of the founding of the monastery: 'Marking the lines for the foundation of the Monastery'

The Hall of the Kings

- *King Dom Afonso Henriques and the five Monks who followed him find the new Monastery marked out in the place where it exists today.*

- *Foundation of the Royal and Illustrious Monastery of Alcobaça on which the King, Dom Afonso Henriques, lays the first stone of the building.*

- Transcribed on a tenth panel, symbolically positioned beneath the Coronation group, are the principal passages of the legend, extracted from the *Chronica de Cister*.

Tiled panel depicting images of the legend of the founding of the monastery: 'Changing the site of the Monastery'

Tiled panel depicting images of the legend of the founding of the monastery: 'King Afonso Henriques lays the first stone'

The Hall of the Kings 101

Terracotta group of the Coronation of King Afonso Henriques, by Pope Alexander III and St Bernard

Terracotta statues of Kings Sancho II and Afonso III

On the upper part of the wall and running around the entire room is a gallery of terracotta portraits of the Kings of Portugal, from Afonso Henriques to José. They were brought here in 1765 from the former Hall of the Kings (now the Hall of Conclusions) and reflect the strong connections linking the Cistercian Order, especially the Autonomous Portuguese Congregation, with the principle of monarchy and the Portuguese royal house. This is spectacularly illustrated in the large composition depicting the 'symbolic' coronation of King Afonso Henriques performed by Pope Alexander III and St Bernard. The tableau of three figures eloquently underlines the crucial contribution of St Bernard and the Cistercians to the foundation and survival of the kingdom of Portugal.

102   The Monastery of Alcobaça

There were originally 23 statues in total, only 19 of which remain. King Afonso VI is represented without his crown because, as Cocheril points out, he was deposed in 1667. The three Spanish kings who occupied the Portuguese throne between 1580 and 1640, when King João IV of Bragança restored the Portuguese monarchy, were never represented. The reason was obvious: the Cistercian cause, both in terms of the Order's own independence and its support of the Portuguese monarchy, could never be served by Spaniards.

The Hall of the Kings

104   The Monastery of Alcobaça

Terracotta statues of
Kings Pedro I, Fernando,
João I and Duarte

Terracotta statue of
King Sebastian

Terracotta statues of
Kings Afonso V, João II
and Manuel

Terracotta statues
of Kings Dinis and
Afonso IV

The Hall of the Kings

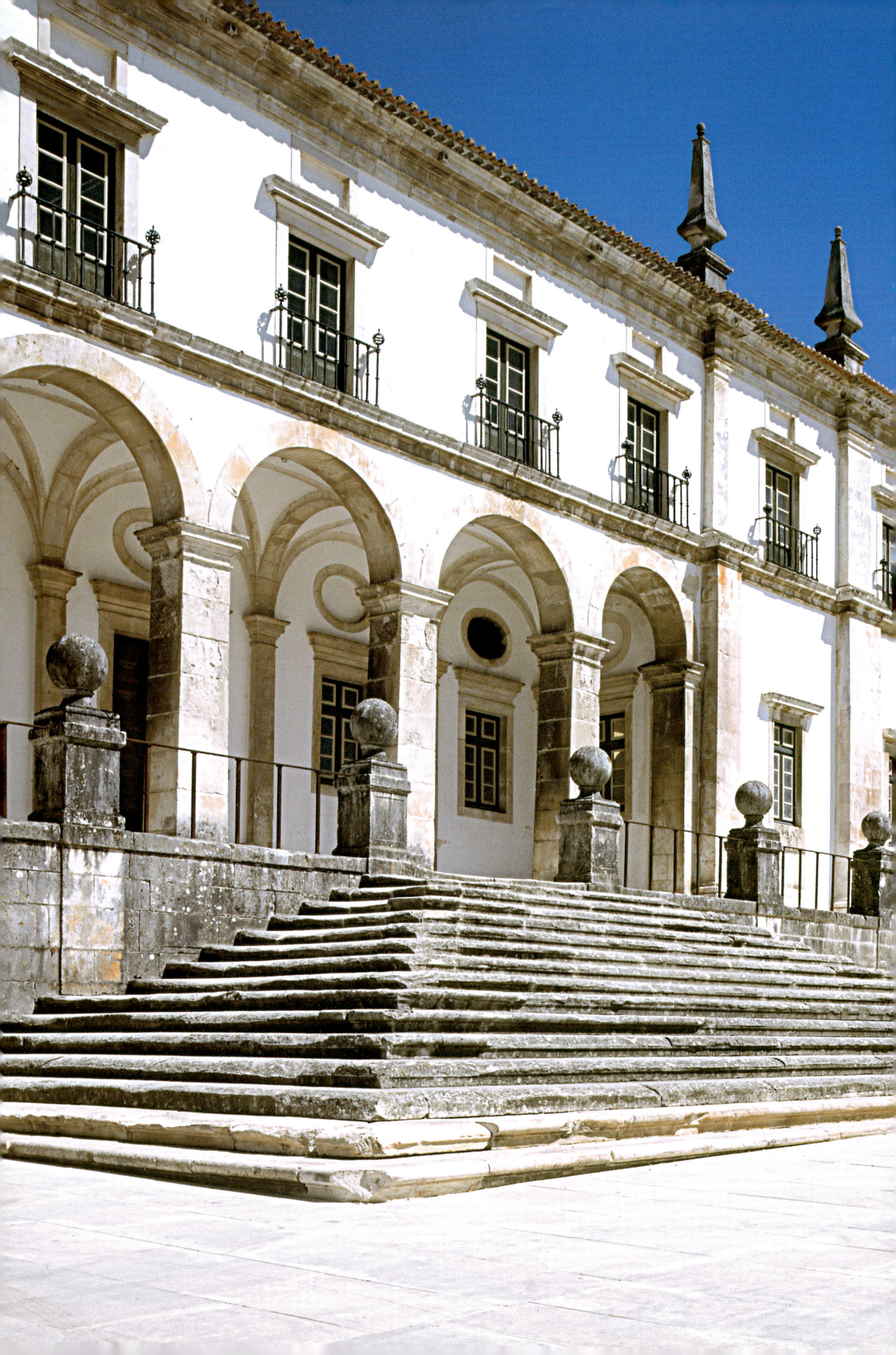

Main entrance to
the Abbot's Palace

THE NEW WINGS

On either side of the church façade, two considerably sized new wings were built. Rafael Moreira attributes the genesis of this project to Friar João Turriano, around 1651 to 1653, during the abbacy of Friar Gerardo Pestana. Each wing possesses an almost symmetrical exterior, creating a palatial appearance similar to noble civil buildings of the seventeenth century,

They are large continuous façades with prominent window arrangements. The ground floor displays large windows with stone mouldings and projecting rectangular pediments. The upper floor has corresponding French windows following the same pattern, also topped by straight pediments, with narrow wrought-iron balconies that sport at their corners the armillary spheres that were common in seventeenth-century palaces.

The façade is broken in two places on the south side – corresponding to the buildings of the College of Nossa Senhora da Conceição and the apartments of the Abbots General of the Autonomous Congregation – by the prominence given to a large window group flanked by pilasters and surmounted by truncated pyramidal pinnacles. Integrated into the area of the monastery that is now a museum, this building is used as a gallery for temporary exhibitions.

The same basic arrangement is followed on the north façade, except at the northwest corner, where a flight of steps gives access to the guest house through a rather noble entrance with a portico. This building, alongside the Hall of the Kings and the Hall of Conclusions, and positioned between the portico entrance and the present Hall of the Kings constituted the set of seventeenth-century additions to the ground floor, with the guest accommodation extending onto the upper floor. These replaced the medieval buildings that had previously stood there.

Two small cloisters provide ventilation and light to the interior of this block of rooms. The first of these, known as the Prison Cloister, is smaller and more utilitarian in style. It linked the Hall of Ceremonies and the Hall of Conclusions with the entrance to the Guest House, where the ground floor is open, with large stone arches, and the upper floor closed. The Hall of Conclusions still has a wooden ceiling painted in grotesque from 1675, which has been attributed to Francisco Ferreira Araújo by Vítor Serrão. The second cloister, larger in size and known as the Cloister of Afonso VI, is in the guest house. There is a clear distinction between its two levels: the ground floor, for example, has the same type of semicircular arches as the other cloister, also reinforced on the inside by plain pilasters, while on the upper floor there is a gallery with Tuscan columns standing on pedestals harmoniously integrated into a continuous parapet. The columns support a frieze of classical design, with plain metopes and triglyphs. The whole group is made of stone and establishes a sober but noble and elegant model that is repeated throughout the seventeenth-century additions to the monastery, most of which are situated to the east of the monastic complex.

South wing of the
Exhibition Gallery

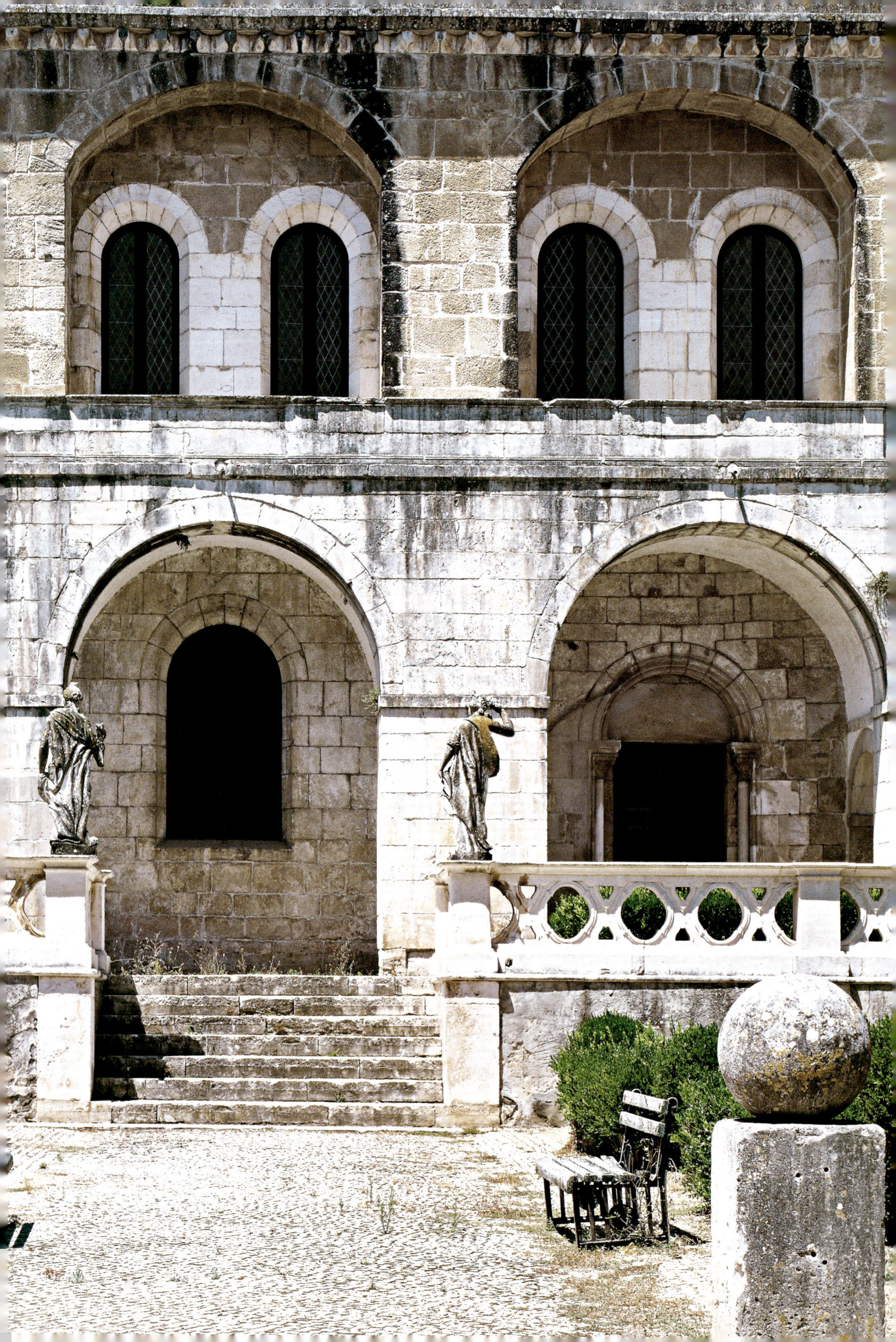

Façade of the Monks' Dormitory, viewed from the Cardinal's Cloister

THE SEVENTEENTH-CENTURY ADDITIONS

The most significant of the seventeenth-century constructions, which added a new set of buildings to the monastic complex, was without doubt the Cardinal's Cloister (*Claustro do Cardeal*), also known as the Novices' Cloister (*Claustro dos Noviços*). Situated to the east of the medieval buildings, it stands adjacent to the large Monks' Dormitory, where it can be seen from the large terrace that runs along the full length of the building.

There may be a number of reasons for the two names given to this building. It is known as the Cardinal's Cloister in homage to the Cardinal-Infante Dom Henrique, the great patron of the Cistercian Monastery of Cós, which is a short distance from Alcobaça. In charge of Alcobaça between 1542 and 1580, he became, in effect, the first monastic administrator of the complex after the establishment of the Autonomous Portuguese Congregation in 1567. Rafael Moreira even claims that the Cardinal may have promoted the building of this cloister after 1548, to a design by Miguel de Arruda, and that its construction may have extended from the end of the sixteenth century well into the seventeenth. Its alternative name (Novices' Cloister) reflects the practical and utilitarian purposes to which it was put, since it was here that the novitiate was moved after these new buildings were completed.

The Cardinal's Cloister, where the new apartments of the abbot general were also built, is a large four-sided space surrounded by porticoes on three sides, with arcades of slightly depressed arches standing on solid, square-section piers. The treatment of the openings and arches is then repeated on the intermediate floor, giving the building the appearance of a double set of porticoes, or a continuous 'loggia' around the three new wings. The design of the piers and arches is similar on both floors, with a stone facing giving a slight relief to the pilasters and soffits of the arches, which spring from simple corbels. A frieze in the same style then links the various arches, with a small accompanying relief, and visually enlivens the external tympana of the cruciform piers. It is a rather sober arrangement but one which demonstrates great architectural nobility. There is also clear evidence of the influence of the 'plain style' that derived from the Spanish 'unornamented style' introduced into Portugal in the period of Spanish dominion under the Felipes.

The top floor, more modest and utilitarian, is in plastered masonry, punctuated by small square windows that follow the pattern of the arcades on the two floors below. These arcades were walled up on the ground floor of the south wing and filled in with modern windows on the intermediate floor of the north wing. Here, marking the transverse axis of the cloister, is a mansard structure topped by a triangular pediment. The French windows at this level and also on the upper floor, as on the opposite side, mark the line along which the monastery's watercourse ran – a large canal lined with stone know as the *levada*.

The only wing of this cloister to have a façade of a different kind is on the side of the medieval monastery or, more specifically, of the large Monks' Dormitory. It was given a more noble treatment, with non-communicating stone arches that are larger in dimension than those of the other wings, and through which, because they are not very deep, you can see the wall, doors and windows of the original construction. A large terrace was built on the first floor, which can be accessed from the dormitory.

The whole courtyard was treated as a garden, with a higher section offering a narrow terrace and four decorative classical-style statues on the same west side. Further down there is a formal garden of boxwood

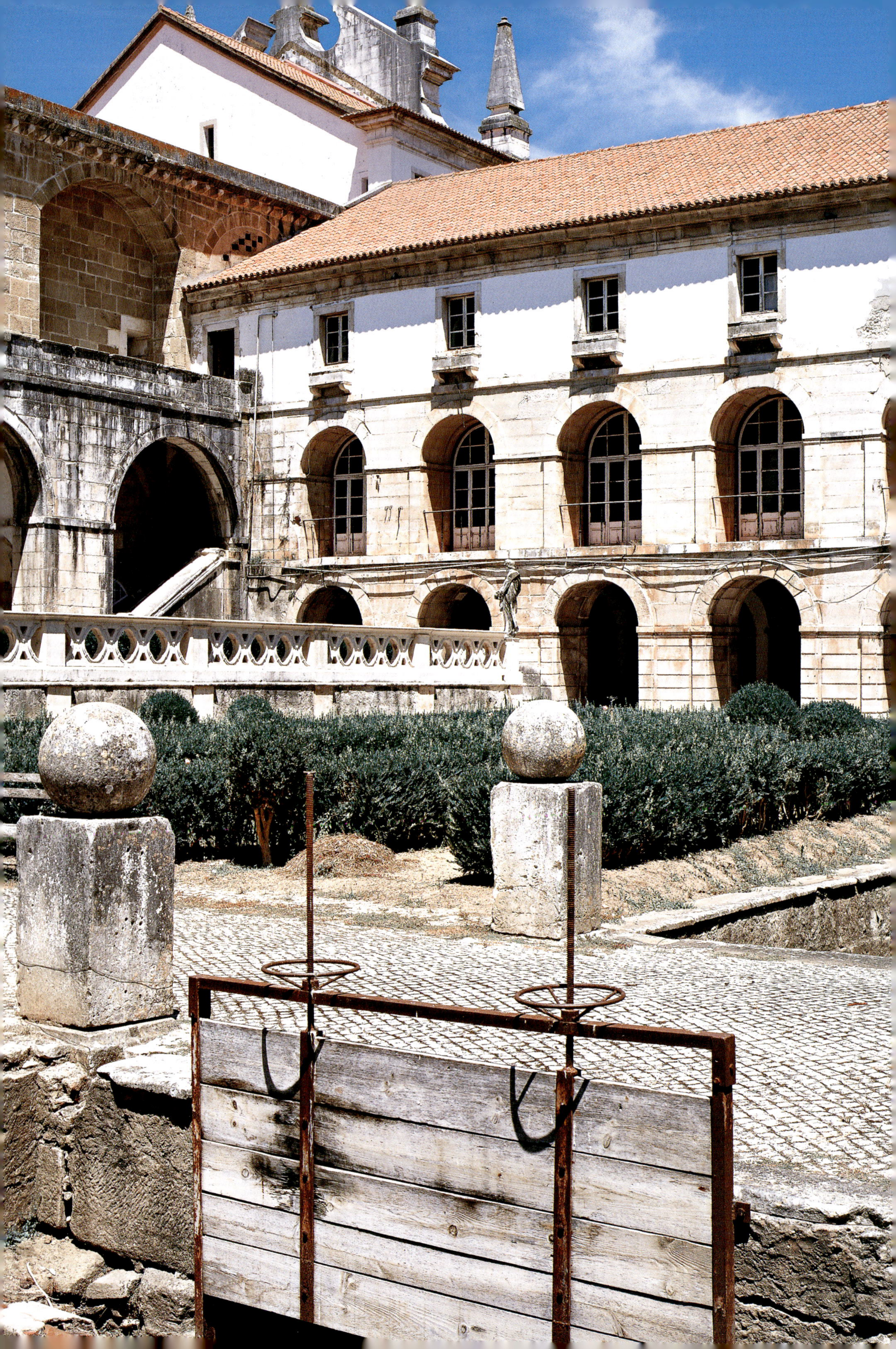

The Cardinal's Cloister, looking south to the *levada*

The Cardinal's Cloister

hedges divided into four parts along the longitudinal axis – defined by the steps that go down from the medieval part of the monastery, passing over the watercourse along a bridge with four pillars topped by spherical shapes – and, transversely, by the watercourse itself.

The buildings around this cloister served various functions: the north and east sections housed the novices, with the cells opening onto broad corridors; and the south side, a good deal narrower, was essentially a passageway from the novices' quarters to the church, and provided access to the buildings further to the east.

The interior structure of the wings includes porticoes on the ground floor, which are similar in many ways to the geometry of the corridors themselves, but which have very elaborate stone ornamentation. Double semicircular arches springing from corbels on quadrangular pilasters, both on the courtyard side and on the interior wall, are accompanied by an intrados (also in stone) for the full length of the piers. This arrangement gives a sense of harmony and visual vitality to the whole, which is further reinforced by the stone ribs of the groin vaults in each bay of the various wings, where the lime-washed white of the walls and vault contrasts with the dark stone of the piers, pilasters, consoles and arches.

The structure is essentially repeated on the upper floor but the bays have a flat ceiling in place of the crossed-rib vaults.

The Seventeenth-Century Additions

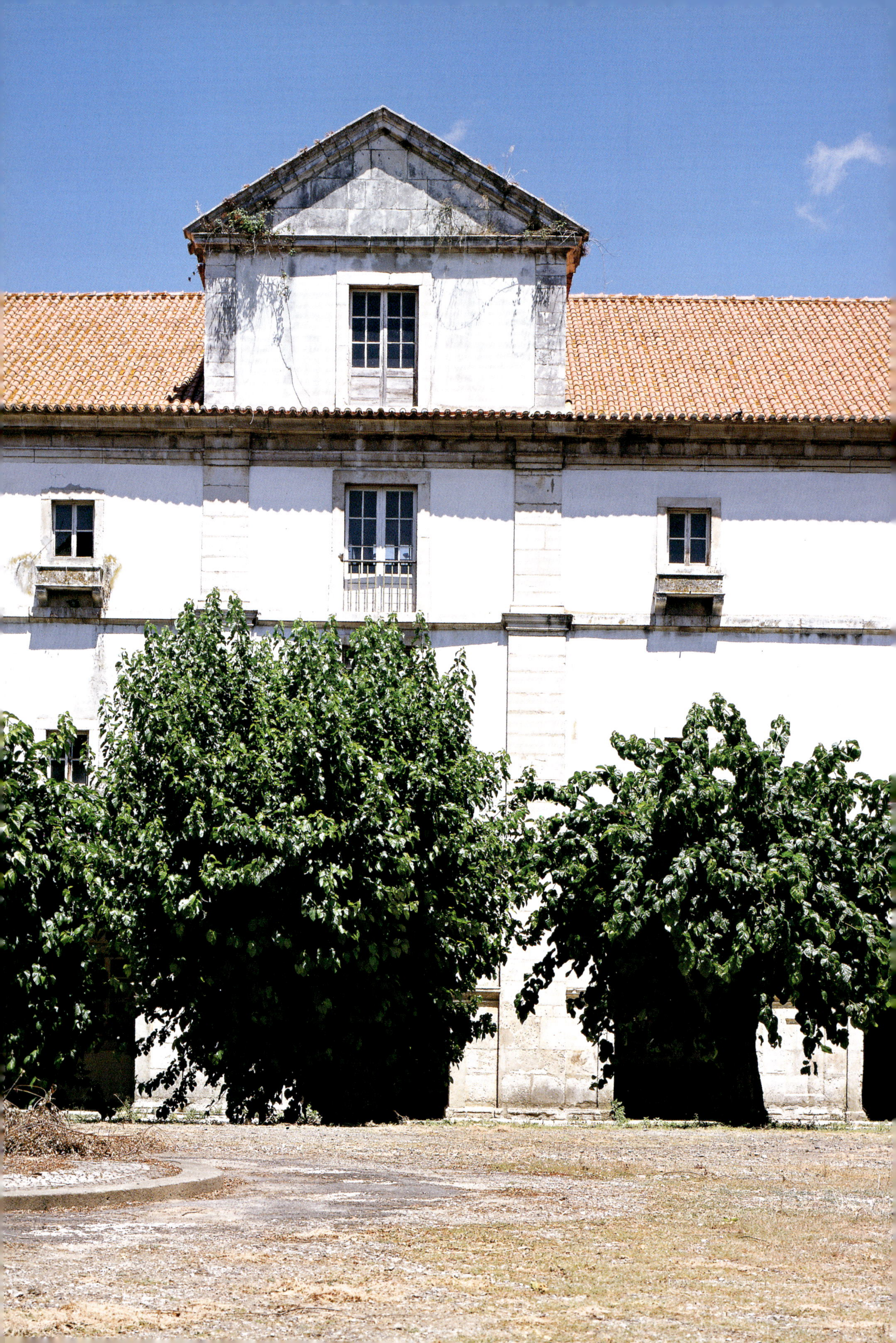

The Woodcutting Cloister

THE WOODCUTTING CLOISTER

Following on from and to the east of the Cardinal's Cloister is the Woodcutting Cloister (*Claustro do Rachadoiro*) or Library Cloister (*Claustro da Biblioteca*), squarer and slightly larger than the previous one but essentially following the architectural and decorative features common in buildings of this period.

The cloister's name indicates its utilitarian function. It was here, on the ground floor, that the saddlery, woodwork and bookbinding workshops were located, as well as some of the storerooms. It was also where the wood was chopped for heating purposes and to supply the workshops and kitchen.

The monastery archives were kept in a large vaulted room on the upper floor, while the large library (hence its alternative name) was located in the south wing, which has a distinctive exterior decoration.

On the ground floor, the elevation of the four wings is identical to that in the Cardinal's Cloister, with the same stone arches defining a gallery with porticoes that formerly ran all the way around the construction. Following successive alterations this gallery is no longer intact, having been largely walled up and altered on the west side, with the arches on the south side also bricked up and several curious oculi having been set into the walls to provide light for the corridor, which is now interior.

The wings of the first floor also mirror those of the Cardinal's Cloister, with the same type of arches, corbels and pilasters. However, the vaulting of the various bays, which is also groined, is missing the stone ribs of its nobler predecessor, no doubt reflecting the more functional nature of this building.

The same effect is evident in the elevation of the various wings, with the two upper floors following a similar composition: both are closed, made of plastered and lime-washed masonry, and pierced with rectangular windows with stone mouldings, following the pattern of the arches of the ground floor. On the roof, three mansard structures similar to the one in the Novices' Cloister mark the dominant axes, two on the north and south wings and one on the east wing.

The interior of these wings is identical to the previous cloister, with the same walls and openings. The only exception appears in the south wing, on the level corresponding to the *piano nobile (*or main floor), where the three doors that open from the corridor to the southern constructions are rather curious.

The door in the centre of the wing has very elaborate stone moulding with dripstones on the upper part. It is flanked by, and provides an interesting contrast with, two broad pilasters in bas-relief facing the lime-washed wall. This door leads to the stairs down to the Obelisk Garden (*Jardim do Obelisco*) in the centre of the southern façade of the complex.

On either side of this door are another two doorways, similar in ornamentation but without the pilasters that lend nobility to the central one. Behind this façade, in the south wing, is the library, which is accessible via a side wing. The doors here are decorated in a similar fashion but without the dripstones, indicating its more functional nature.

Finally, on the north side, is the exterior façade of this group – the Cardinal's Cloister and the Woodcutting Cloister – which basically follows the model of the buildings on the west side and of the interior of the Library Cloister: three floors, the lower one being closed off, with false arcades, and the two upper floors having large rectangular windows with stone mouldings. The mansard roof has curbs at

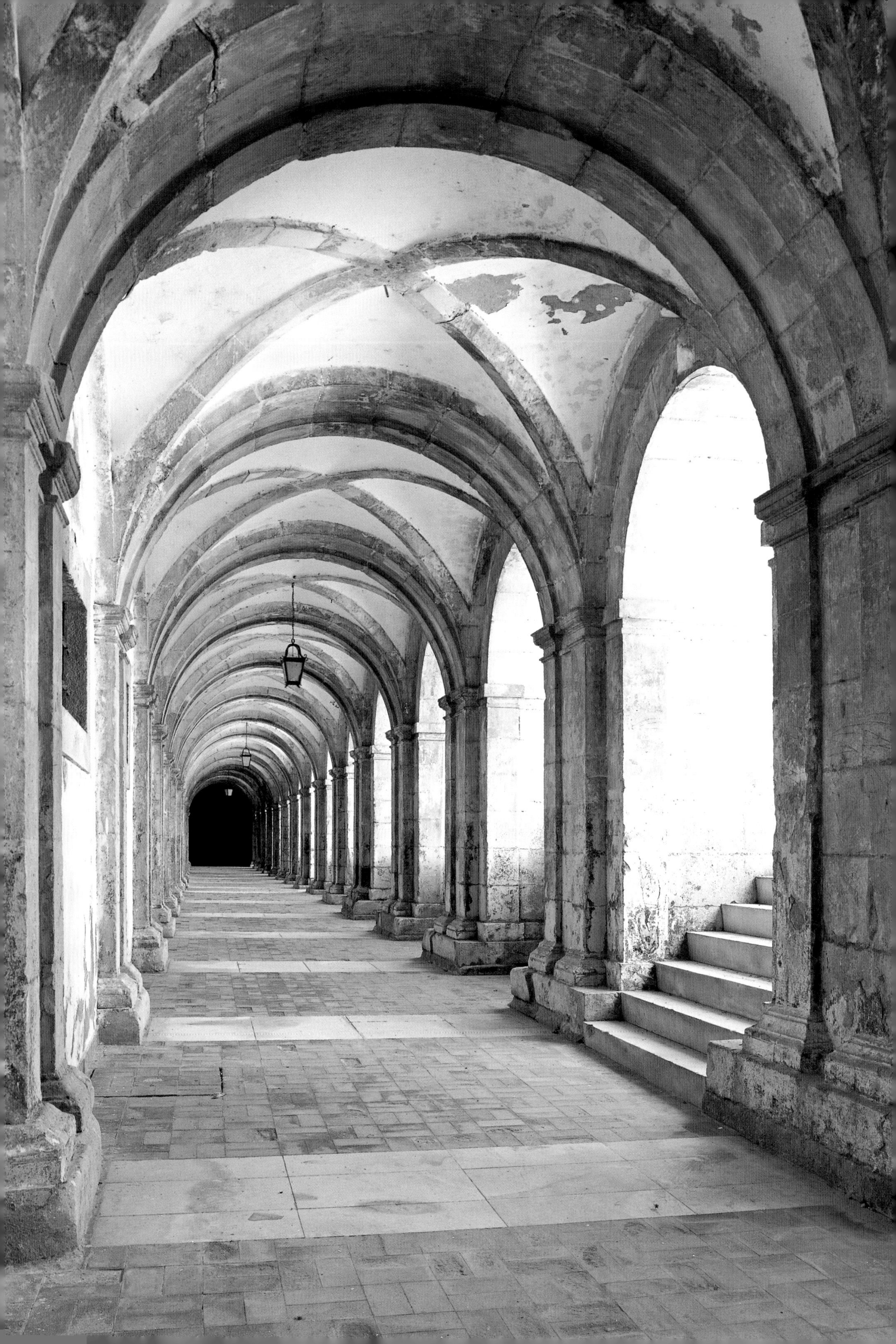

Ground floor gallery of the Woodcutting Cloister

Façade of the library in the south wing of the Woodcutting Cloister

regular intervals topped with triangular pediments similar to those on the interior façades. The overall impression is one of great sobriety and a certain classicism, while also stressing that this part of the monastery was largely given over to secular activities. The set of exterior façades of the Cardinal's Cloister and Woodcutting Cloister form – along with those of the kitchen, refectory and former guests' quarters – an extensive and imposing stretch of wall, continuing irregularly for over 100 metres.

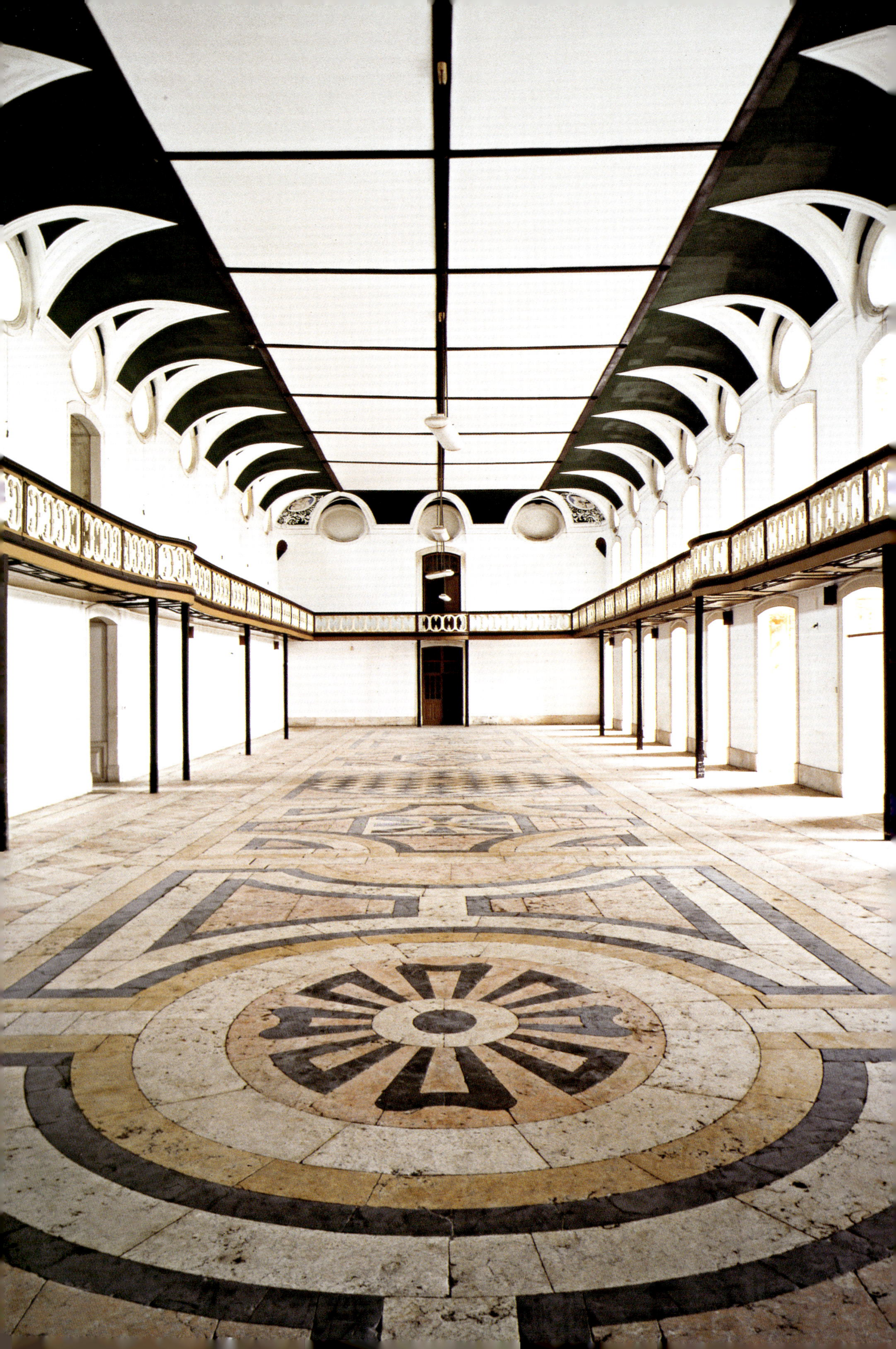

Interior of the library

THE LIBRARY

Situated on the third floor of the south wing of the Woodcutting Cloister, and looking out over the Obelisk Garden, the great library is one of the most interesting rooms of the new wings.

Almost 50 metres long and nearly 13 metres wide, it is where the monks consulted the precious codices and books of the bibliographical collection that had been built up by the monastery since the thirteenth century. This came to an abrupt end with the suppression of the religious orders in Portugal by decree of Joaquim António de Aguiar in 1834. These valuable collections were then integrated into the national archive, which, in the case of the scripts from the Monastery of Alcobaça, are kept in the reserved section of the National Library in Lisbon. The collection includes over 300 medieval codices, many of them richly illuminated, from the former monastic scriptorium.

The main hall of the library has a very high ceiling and is lit by two long rows of 11 large windows, facing south, and by 22 oval oculi at the level of the interior of the roof. Eleven of these match the rhythm of the large windows, while the other 11 repeat the pattern, but are facing north. Three similar oval oculi, blind in this case, adorn the east and west ends, maintaining the pattern created by those on the other walls.

The large windows on the lower floor have wide embrasures, open from top to bottom, while those on the upper floor are accessible through a wooden gallery that runs around the room, with a decorated wood balustrade. The whole construction dates from the second half of the eighteenth century. The gallery and several decorative paintings on the inside of the arched embrasures around the lower windows suggest that it may have been completed in the early nineteenth century.

According to Cocheril, the decoration in the library would have been very rich and colourful. A large central ceiling medallion would have been surrounded by elaborate ornamentation, representing, in *mezzo rilievo*, the figure of St Bernard surrounded by flowers, along with various emblems and symbols. This ceiling, the only record of which exists in old photographs, finally collapsed as a result of rainwater damage due to a failure to maintain the roofs. Of the original scheme, only the four corner medallions, in painted stucco, remain. They depict the four Evangelists – St John, St Luke, St Mark and St Matthew – as well as some curious ribbon decorations that surround the oval oculi, also in stucco or clay, the background having been repainted at a later date.

Of the remaining original decoration, the most noteworthy is the remarkable flooring in inlaid marble – using white, black, pink and yellow varieties –, which is laid in highly elaborate geometric patterns covering the entire surface. The floor, like the dripstones in this wing, is reminiscent of the most magnificent Portuguese Baroque building of the century, the great complex of the Palace and Convent of Mafra.

Other decorative features consist of motifs painted in soft colours, which have become seriously faded with time. They feature on all the intradoses of the window embrasures on the ground floor, with delicate mouldings of garlands, festoons and fanciful cartouches. At their centres are highly naturalistic polychrome depictions of landscapes, bucolic and frequently exotic, showing birds, ships, cities and rural scenes. From their formal characteristics they appear to be works from the late eighteenth or possibly the early nineteenth centuries.

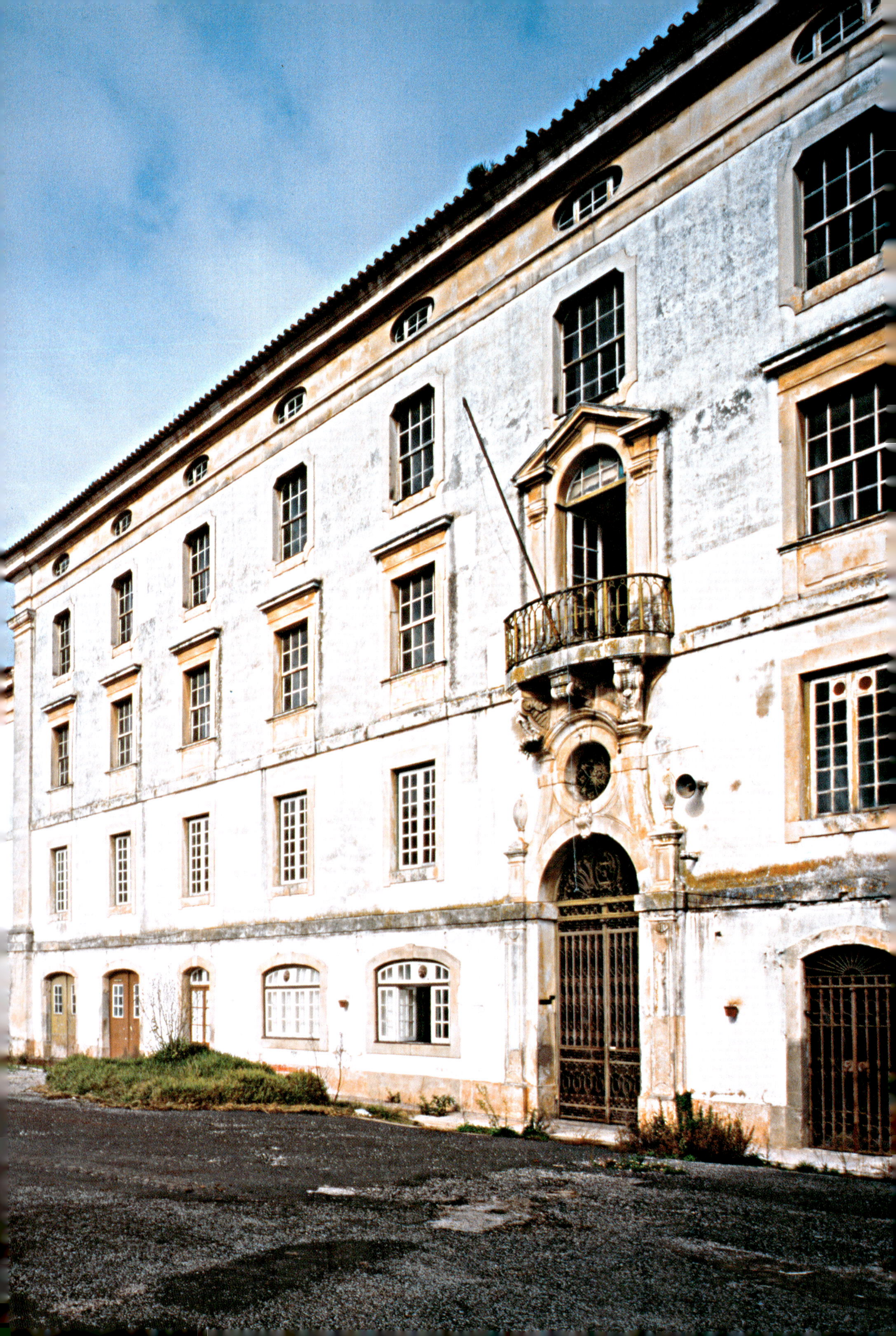

Façade of the library

THE OBELISK GARDEN

On the south side of the Library Cloister the Obelisk Garden extends over a broad area of the rear eastern part of the monastery enclosure, its two most important constructions being the façade of the library and the obelisk itself.

The façade of the library, like most of the façades of the new wings of the monastery, has a distinctly palatial look, the difference here being that it is a work of the second half of the eighteenth century, strongly influenced by the great construction of Mafra.

Viewed from the garden, it is a façade with four levels clearly marked by large windows, topped by a further string of oval windows – those of the library – cut in the cornice immediately below the roof. Although the windows on the ground floor, with a moulding topped by a very depressed arch, reflect the utilitarian nature of the rooms, in which workshops and storerooms were located, the two upper floors are more distinctive.

Thus, those on the first floor have straight stone lintels, which protrude only slightly and which have a small decorative motif on the corners of the lower parapet.

Those on the floor above are false bay windows, since the parapet faces the wall. Their prominent feature is the straight pediment, in relief, on their upper part.

Marking the dominant central axis of the façade, which has 11 sets of windows at various levels, there is an arrangement that clearly derives from the Baroque approach of the Joanine period (the reign of King João V). There is a portal of curved mouldings extended by an oval oculus on the first floor, and above that, on the *piano nobile* – and without any interruption in the marble moulding of the overall scheme – a large French window with its corresponding narrow balcony surmounted by a triangular pediment standing on lateral pilasters. The great nobility of this design adds to the dynamism of the façade. The door, as well as the window of the *piano nobile*, boasts the characteristic Mafra-style dripstones.

The originality of the entire façade is reinforced by the large rectangular windows of the upper floor, whose corners are cut off to create octagons in another typically Joanine design; and, finally, by the scheme of the oval oculi, which follows the pattern of the openings in the lower levels.

As the part of the complex displaying the most Baroque features, the Obelisk Garden still retains some vestiges of its original grandeur.

Water for the monastery is obtained from here, from the watercourse that draws from the rivers that gave the town its name – the Alcôa and the Baça rivers.

Three of the fountains that originally decorated the garden still exist. They are characteristically Baroque, with backs made of decorated stone and original green glazed tiles with a metallic sheen. The stone decoration invokes fanciful and naturalistic themes. One of the fountains is still clearly visible from inside the library, while the others are further south, along the wall that divided the Obelisk Garden from the adjacent Myrtle Garden and from the former cemetery. One of these is situated on the outside of the present boundary wall, on the bend that divides the watercourse where it enters the monastery.

The garden's most attractive feature is its centrally placed obelisk, from which it takes its name. It is one of the most interesting Baroque artefacts of the entire eighteenth-century section of the monastery.

Taking the shape of a pyramidal frustum, the obelisk is decorated with ornamental protrusions placed at regular intervals. It stands on a tall parallelepiped pedestal decorated with masks on all four sides. Rising to a simple unadorned point, it stands in a large oval artificial lake surrounded by a stone wall. It could have provided the setting for fountains or other water features so popular during the Baroque era, or it might simply have been the focal point of an area of rest and recreation for a monastic community, which, by that time, had strayed far from St Bernard's principles of austerity and restraint.

Detail of masks at the base of the obelisk

The obelisk

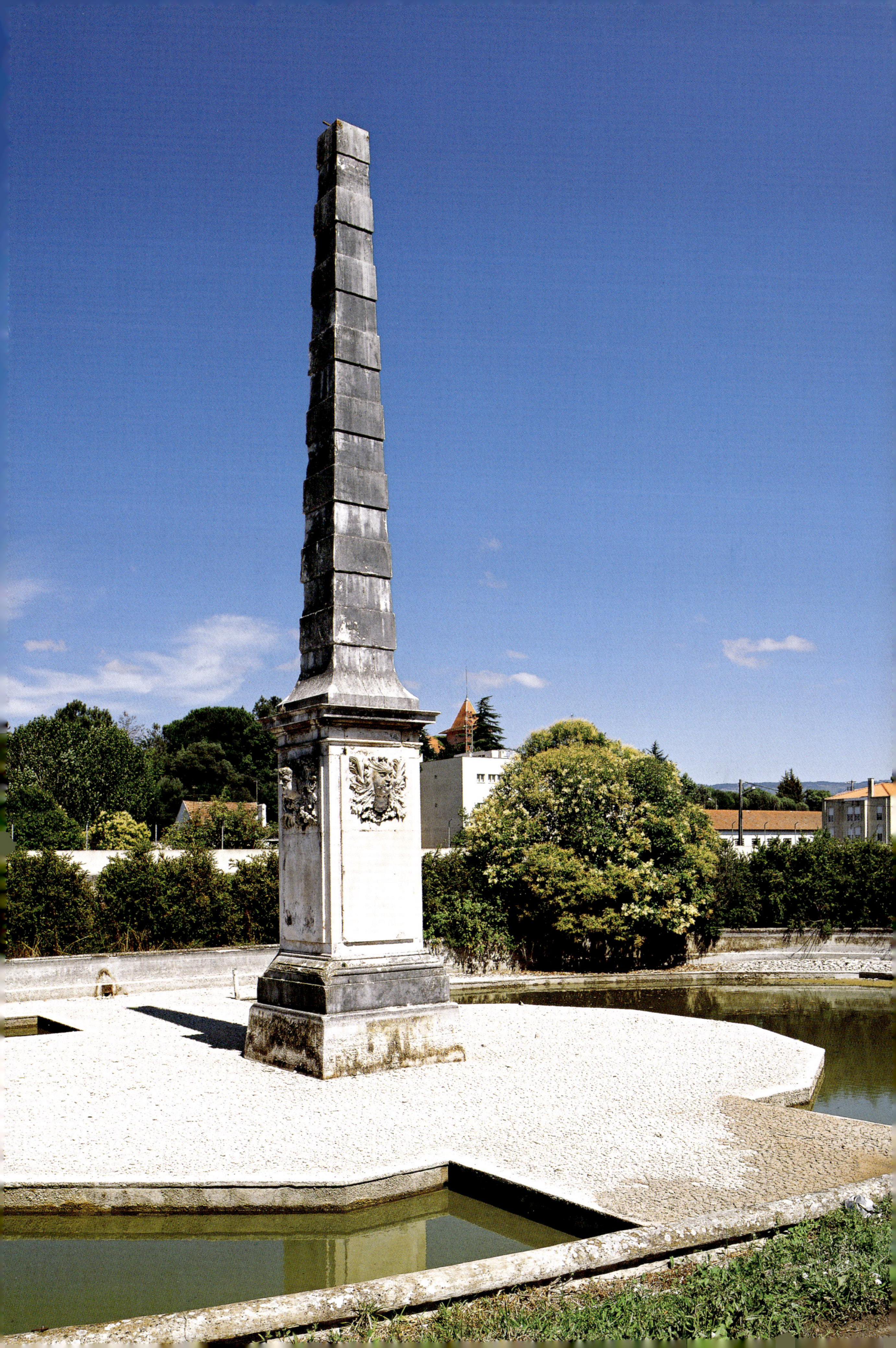

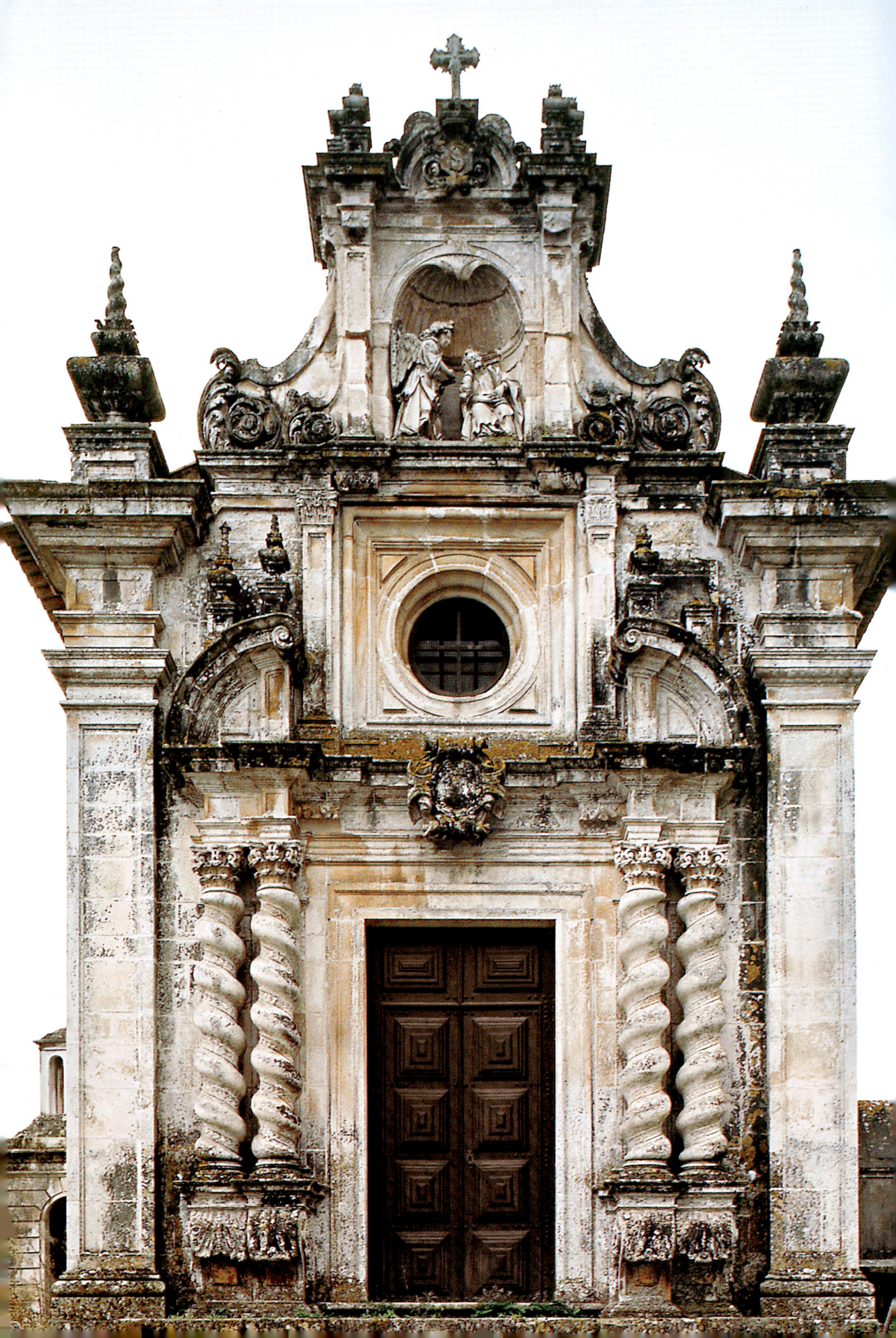

THE MYRTLE GARDEN AND CHAPEL OF EXILE

Adjacent to the Obelisk Garden, on the west side, is the Myrtle Garden. It was here that the Chapel of Our Lady of Exile (or simply the Chapel of Exile) was built in the first quarter of the eighteenth century, on the site of the cemetery.

The theme of exile is a recurrent one among the Cistercians of the Autonomous Portuguese Congregation and one frequently represented in its monasteries. As well as at Alcobaça, a Chapel of Exile was erected in the monastery precincts at Santa Maria de Salzedas, with eighteenth-century *azulejos* recounting the story known as the Flight to Egypt. At Santa Maria do Bouro, the theme of exile is represented on the façade by an image of Jesus positioned between the Virgin Mary and St Joseph, which was known as the Return from Egypt. It reoccurs in another Cistercian monastery at São João de Tarouca, in a similar sculptural group on the altar of Our Lady of Exile. This representation lies alongside that of another gallery of Portuguese monarchs which again excludes the three Spanish kings called Felipe.

Exile was, for the Cistercians of the Autonomous Congregation, one of the touchstones of their identification with the plight of the Portuguese monarchy. They closely followed the monarchy's forced exclusion from power during the period of Spanish rule, and their return after 1640 with the Restoration. Having collaborated in the founding of Portugal through St Bernard's recognition of King Afonso Henriques as monarch, they were in alliance, from the seventeenth century onwards, with its re-establishment. By that point the secular theme of the galleries of the Portuguese monarchs complemented the religious theme of the Return from Egypt. According to Luís de Moura Sobral, the return to the Promised Land mirrored the legitimisation of the royal power of the new dynasty, the Braganças.

This is reflected in a large part of the bibliographical output of Alcobaça, which was distinctly historical in nature. It was here that the first part of the *Monarchia Lusitana* was printed, using a typography established by the monks at the end of the sixteenth century. The *Geographia Antiga de Lusytania* by Friar Bernardo de Brito, and the tiny *Officium Feriale Sanctissimi Patris Nostri Bernardi* were among the other works to be printed here.

The Cistercians were highly interested in studying historical matters relating to the kingdom and the Lusitanian monarchy, and they even set up a group of researchers, supported by successive abbots general, known as the Chroniclers of Alcobaça. The head chroniclers or historians of the Order (men whose task it was to write down the chronicles of the kings and of the kingdom) lay the foundations for the establishment of this group. One of these was Friar Bernardo de Brito (1569–1617), who, after the death of the head chronicler Francisco de Andrade, occupied the post until his own death, and whose most important legacy was to start the *Monarchia Lusitana*. This work was completed by notable Cistercians such as Friar António Brandão (1584–1637), Friar Francisco Brandão (1601–80), Friar Manoel dos Santos (1672–1740), Friar Manuel da Rocha (1676–1744) and Friar Fortunato de São Boaventura (1778–1845).

The Chapel of Exile at Alcobaça was constructed as a small, rectangular building with an exuberant Baroque façade designed as an altarpiece. It has a portal flanked by two twisted columns on either side, topped by a broken segmental pediment. At the centre is an oval oculus, and the whole structure is crowned by an aedicule with a sculptural group depicting the Annunciation.

Interior of the
Chapel of Exile

Interior of the
Chapel of Exile

The interior contains a carved wooden high altar presenting a set of six panels of elaborately detailed glazed tiles; they can be dated to around 1720–23 and are attributed to António Vital Rifarto.

The four panels of the nave, covering the side walls up to the ceiling, depict various passages from the cycle of the Flight to Egypt, while the two on the side walls of the chancel, with passages from the Life of Jesus, are more intimately related to the specific theme of exile, invoking the period after the Return from Egypt. An inscription, repeated on these two panels, reads, *Hic est filius meus dilectus* (This is my beloved son).

Following page
Main façade of
the monastery

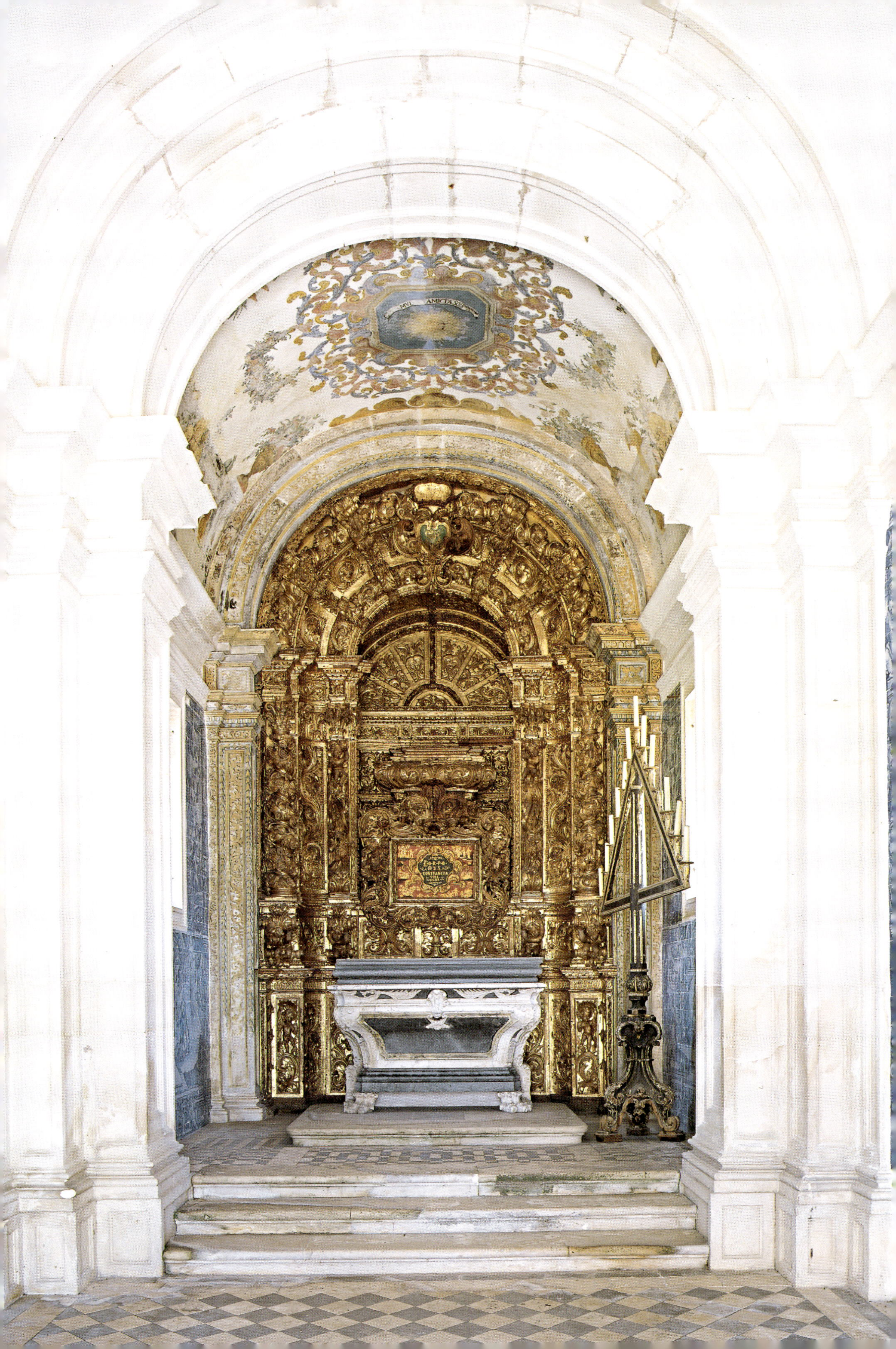

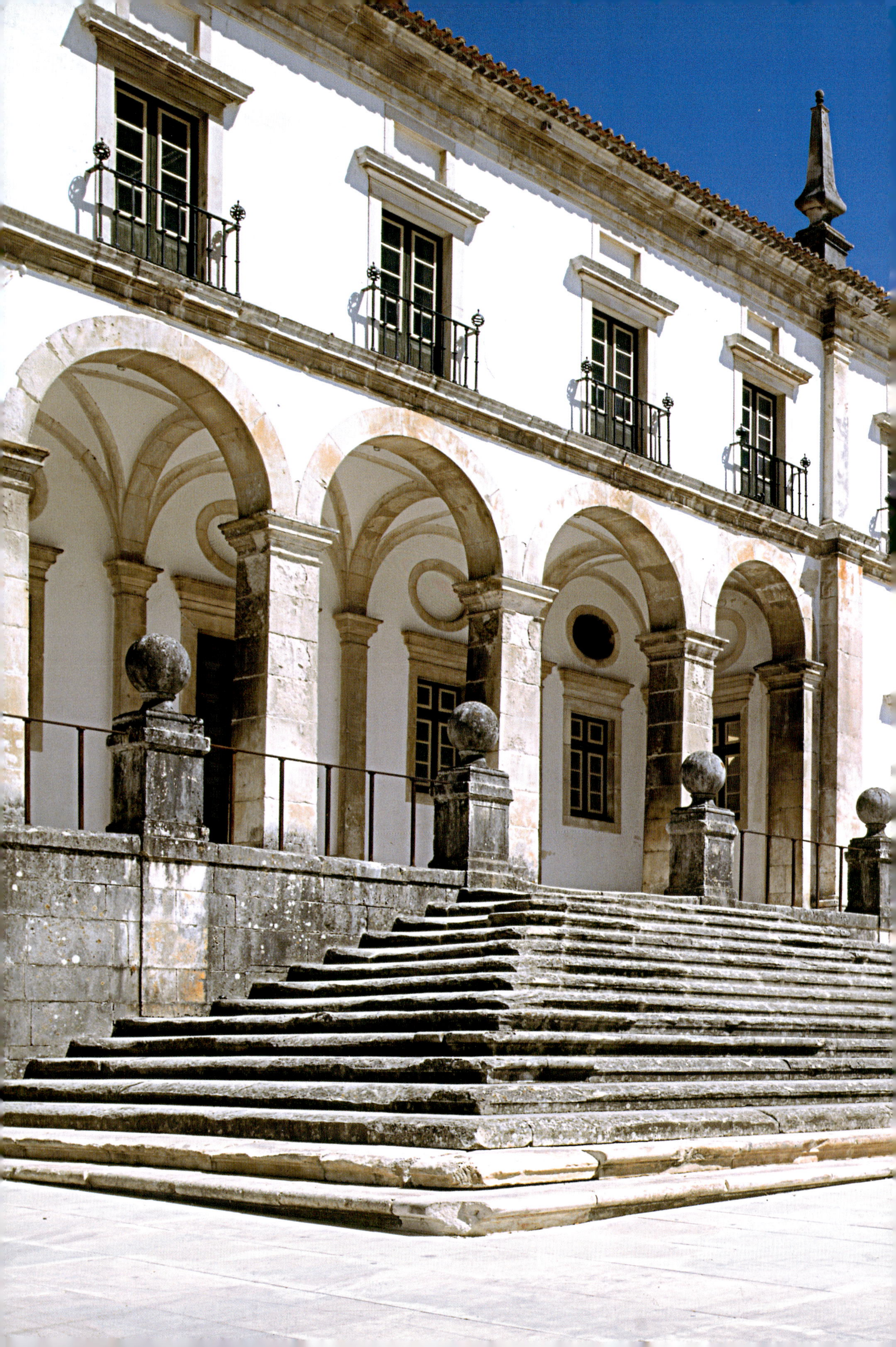

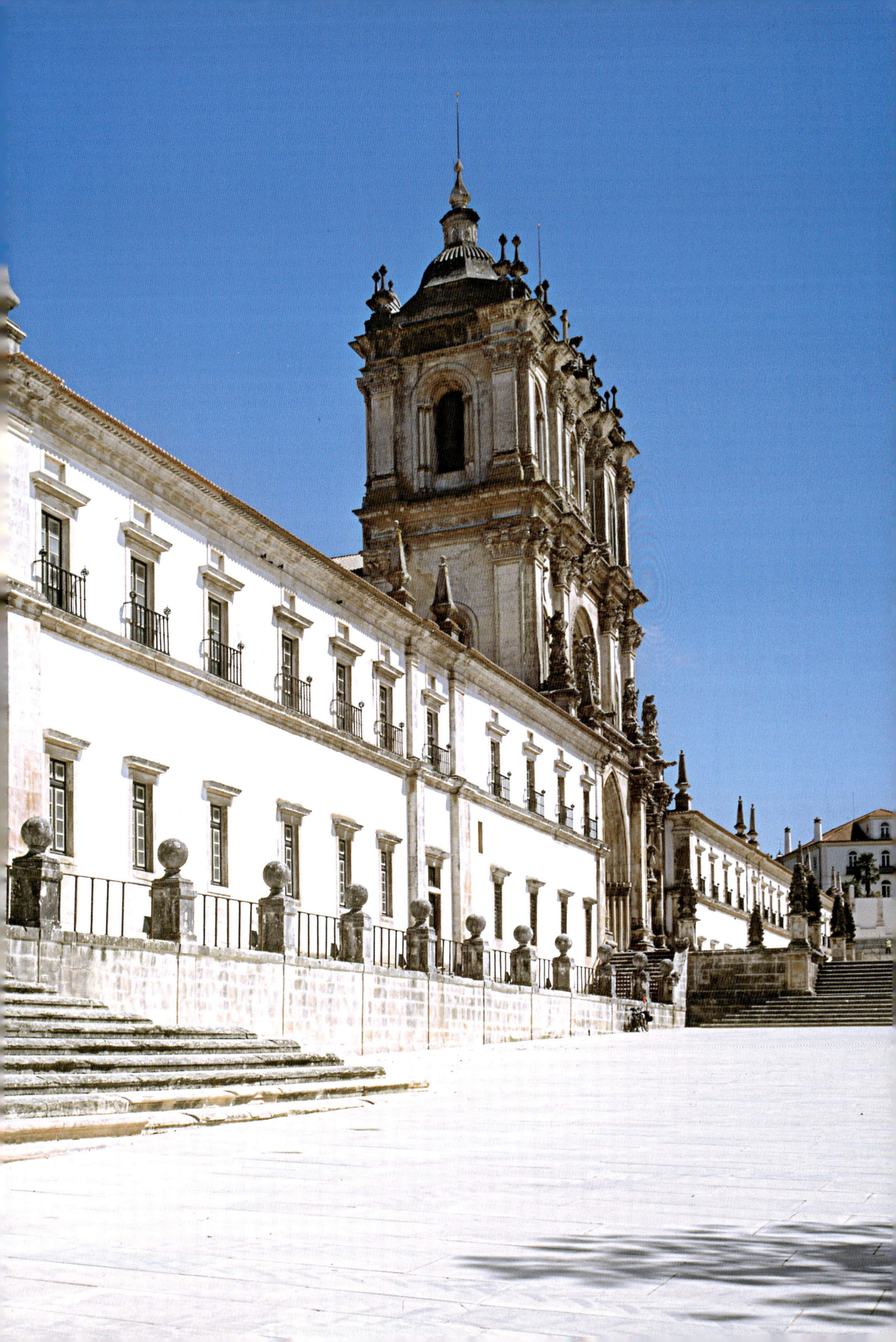

BIBLIOGRAPHY

ALMEIDA, Carlos Alberto Ferreira de, 'O Românico', in *História da Arte em Portugal*, vol. 3, Lisbon, Publicações Alfa, 1986.

ALMEIDA, Fortunato de, *História da Igreja em Portugal*, 4 vols., Barcelos, Portucalense Ed., 1967-70.

Arte de Cister em Portugal e Galiza (Exhibition Catalogue), Lisbon, Fundação Calouste Gulbenkian and Fundación Pedro Barrié de la Maza, 1998.

Arte e Arquitectura nas Abadias Cistercienses nos séculos XVI, XVII e XVIII (Conference Proceedings), Lisbon, IPPAR, 2000.

Arte Sacra nos Antigos Coutos de Alcobaça (Exhibition Catalogue), Lisbon, IPPAR, 1995.

BOAVENTURA, Frei Fortunato de, *História Cronológica e Crítica da Real Abadia de Alcobaça*, Lisbon, 1827.

Cister: Espaços, Territórios, Paisagens (International Conference Proceedings), 2 vols., Lisbon, IPPAR, 2000.

COCHERIL, Maur, *Alcobaça. Abadia cisterciense de Portugal*, Lisbon, IN-CM, 1989.

COCHERIL, Maur, *Routier des Abbayes cisterciennes du Portugal*, Paris, Fundação Calouste Gulbenkian, 1978.

CORREIA, Virgílio, 'Uma descrição quinhentista do Mosteiro de Alcobaça', in *O Instituto*, vol. 77, Coimbra, 1929.

DIAS, Pedro, *A Arquitectura Gótica Portuguesa*, Lisbon, Estampa, 1994.

GOMES, Saul António, *Visitações a Mosteiros Cistercienses em Portugal*, Lisbon, IPPAR, 1998.

GOULÃO, Maria José and MACEDO, Francisco Pato, 'Les tombeaux de Pedro et Inês: la mémoire sacralisée d'un amour clandestin', in *Memory and Oblivion: proceedings of the 29th International Congress of the History of Art*, Doordrecht, Kluwer Academic Publishers, 1999, pp. 491-498.

GUSMÃO, Artur Nobre de, *A expansão da arquitectura borgonhesa e os Mosteiros de Cister em Portugal: ensaio de arqueologia da Idade Média*, Lisbon, 1956.

GUSMÃO, Artur Nobre de, *A Real Abadia de Alcobaça: estudo histórico-arqueológico*, Lisbon, Horizonte, 1992.

JORGE, Virgolino, 'Measurement and Number in the Cistercian Church of Alcobaça', in *Arte Medieval*, 2nd series, year VIII, no. 1, vol. 2, Rome, 1994.

MARQUES, Maria Alegria, *Estudos sobre a Ordem de Cister em Portugal*, Lisbon, Colibri, 1998.

MOREIRA, Rafael, 'A encomenda artística em Alcobaça no século XVI', in *Arte Sacra nos Antigos Coutos de Alcobaça* (Exhibition Catalogue), Lisbon, IPPAR, 1995, pp. 40-63.

MOURA, Carlos, 'A escultura maneirista e barroca em Alcobaça: "Escola" ou arte de recepção?', in *Arte Sacra nos Antigos Coutos de Alcobaça* (Exhibition Catalogue), Lisbon, IPPAR, 1995, pp. 64-81.

MOURA, Carlos, 'Da figuração à decoração. O percurso artístico dos mosteiros cistercienses em Portugal entre os séculos XVI e XVIII', in *Arte de Cister em Portugal e Galiza* (Exhibition Catalogue), Lisbon, Fundação Calouste Gulbenkian and Fundación Pedro Barrié de la Maza, 1998, pp. 328-375.

PEREIRA, Paulo (dir.), *História da Arte Portuguesa*, Lisbon, Círculo de Leitores, 1995.

REAL, Manuel Luís, 'A construção cisterciense em Portugal durante a Idade Média', in *Arte de Cister em Portugal e Galiza* (Exhibition Catalogue), Lisbon, Fundação Calouste Gulbenkian and Fundación Pedro Barrié de la Maza, 1998, pp. 42-97.

SERRÃO, Vítor, 'A arte da pintura entre o gótico final e o barroco', in *Arte Sacra nos Antigos Coutos de Alcobaça* (Exhibition Catalogue), Lisbon, IPPAR, 1995, pp. 82-113.

SOBRAL, Luís de Moura, 'Narrativa, história e mito em Santa Maria do Bouro', in *Arte de Cister em Portugal e Galiza* (Exhibition Catalogue), Lisbon, Fundação Calouste Gulbenkian and Fundación Pedro Barrié de la Maza, 1998, pp. 432-465.

SOBRAL, Luís de Moura, 'A Capela do Desterro de Alcobaça: estilo, narração e simbolismo', in *Cister: Espaços, Territórios, Paisagens* (Proceedings of International Conference), vol. II, Lisbon, IPPAR, 2000, pp. 407-424.

VIEIRA DA SILVA, José Custódio, *O Panteão Régio do Mosteiro de Alcobaça*, Lisbon, IPPAR, 2003.

VILLA NOVA, Bernardo, *O Mosteiro de Alcobaça*, Lisbon, 1947.